Grandmother's Footsteps

"Did I tell You I went to India?"

Braiswick

This is the first of the
Grandmother's Footsteps series.

To follow are books on China,
Mexico and who knows where?

"Did I tell You I went to India?"

Grandmother's Footsteps series

Braiswick
61 Gainsborough Road, Felixstowe, Suffolk
IP11 7HS

ISBN 1 898030 29 4

Copyright © 2003 **Jenny McCombe**
www.author.co.uk/mccombe
originally published privately
ISBN : 0 953817 70 9

British Library Cataloguing in Publication
Data available.

Printed in Kent
by JRDigital Print Services Ltd
Braiswick is an imprint of Author Publishing Ltd

ACKNOWLEDGEMENTS

My friends Pete and Sally Ling, Professor Steve Bishop, Anne Macmillan and Ann Johnson-Allen, Trevor Lockwood and everyone who listened when I said: "Did I Tell you I went to India?" and since then have followed in this Grandmother's Footsteps.

ORPHANAGE: if you would like to make a donation send to:

Families for Children
10 Bowling Green
107 Vellalore Road
Pointe Claire
Quebec
Canada

Families for Children
Podanur
Coimbatore 6411 023
Southern India

or to:

Jen Risdale
Virginia House
Jackson Road
Newbourne
Woodbridge IP12 4NR
Suffolk
England

Contents

FOREWORD

When sponsors of a third world orphanage asked me if I would like to be "mum" to 500+ orphans, I didn't know (whether to laugh or cry). How could a 56- year old granny help hundreds of Indian children, many of who have physical and learning disabilities? In the end there was really only one answer - I'd have to go and have a look. I 'd had the sort of experience every mum, grandmother and social worker has had and I thought this experience would be useful in an institution in England but could it benefit these Indian children? I had heard from different sources about a charity called Families for Children, in Southern India, run by a friend of a friend, Jen Risdale, in tandem with some Canadians.

Jen lives in a nearby village in Suffolk and fosters English boys who have been thrown out of their own homes. She also raises money for an Indian orphanage and persuades people to sponsor these children in Tamil Nadu. I happened to see her exhibition of photographs of the Orphanage, while visiting the Unitarian Church in Ipswich. The photographs headed up an appeal for sponsors for the children, who all looked well and happy and very appealing. I was told it cost £10 per month to feed and educate one child - aged from a small baby to a teenager. Families for Children are also an Adoption Agency, arranging for disabled children to go to live with Canadians and Americans but they also provide home, food and education for hundreds of Indian children, in a village called Podenur. They have been doing this for twenty years. They admit new children every week and only lose a few each May when those who are fourteen

1

or so and have any family, return to work and contribute to their families' income. Jen fed me enough information about the project for me to feel no apprehension or nervousness about my possible adventure, and reassured me as to my 'usefulness'. She visited India every year and would join me in April or May. I just started to feel a wonderful anticipation of an adventure, without any real knowledge of what it might really *be* like.

I was at that time living in a wonderful semi-basement flat in town, owned by a good friend who lived in the rest of her Victorian house, upstairs. Hilary had always run the Women's' Refuge in Ipswich and did her usual good job with me, too. I felt I was a refugee from years of married life and *very* rural life, and we joked about my living in her Private Wing but the flat was certainly a heavenly solution to my new circumstances. I had a kitchen window, semi-submerged, looking through her profusion of ferns and flowers and potted plants. Her cats gazed incuriously in at me and seemed to feel the same contentment and relaxation, living there, that I was enjoying. However, I didn't feel so relaxed that I ever wanted to change my mind about going to India. When Jen came to the flat and offered me a year to be a sort of mother to children in the orphanage, primarily the boys, I was absolutely thrilled and couldn't wait to get there.

After I accepted the job it was so interesting observing the reactions of my friends and family to the fact that I was leaving home for so long. Hilary summed up the feelings of my friends, which were primarily anxiety that my living abroad meant they had to write *letters* - with all the time and effort that that entails. Also a feeling of disappointment because I was leaving again, having just become happily involved in their lives and families in the town after many years 'exiled' in the country. One or two of my friends were already jealous of my freedom - from marriage and from work. They told me that they had done some deep thinking about leaving their partners, after Bob (my husband) and I

2

had so successfully split and still remained friends. The job that I was setting off to do was interesting but a bit daunting in some friends' eyes. Lyn would have *loved* to do the work, but Maggie would've loved to do it *if* she could live in a Maharaja's palace while she did it. Fran felt *guilty* that she dare not do such a - in her eyes - brave thing, and Mary felt guilty that she was too contented to do any damn thing at her time of life.

What turned out to be the greatest adventure of my life was the result of an urge to see and experience at first hand more of the lives of foreign people than you get on a holiday. I had to explain to a lot of people here that I was *not* going as the result of a Mother Theresa type urge! There were even friends who told me they felt disturbed and guilty that *they* weren't doing, or at least planning, to do what I was doing, as if I was a Really Good Person and they should be the same. I couldn't seem to get anyone to appreciate the enormous part that Luck was playing in my plans. I am the furthest from a 'Mother Theresa' that you can imagine and my motives were purely selfish in comparison with their interpretation. I was excited because I thought I could live with, and improve the lot of, these boys and girls, in a similar way to the way that I had worked in Suffolk. I hoped that there would be lots of talking, persuading, comforting, organising and improving daily routines of these children. I suppose I anticipated more 'hands on' work in India than social workers experience in England today. I looked forward to less paperwork and knew that if I could find a place to do this work from, I could thoroughly immerse myself in the lives of a completely different people, in a foreign and exotic country, and the possibility made me *buzz*. Luck was playing a huge part in my ability to have this experience, and I couldn't believe how easily the plans evolved.

CHAPTER ONE

In which Grandma Jenny abandons the knitting and heads for foreign parts

I talked about my plans all over my home town of Ipswich, to *everyone* - from the nurse that gave me the relatively few inoculations necessary for India, to the workers in the numerous Indian restaurants that I tried out in Ipswich. They all heard The Lot. The Indians were funny - I would say "I'm off to India next Thursday", and they would say "Oh, do come back and tell us about it when you return - *we've* never been".

Before leaving I had, of course, given a lot of consideration to what I would need for a year in unknown circumstances. I made piles of 'articles' in my bedroom, some to take, some to leave and some to give away. I kept weighing everything on some bathroom scales and spent many happy hours wondering whether "War and Peace" would be better luggage weight value in the long, lonely hours than '1, 000 Crosswords', and whether it was really worth taking my favourite Indian teabags to India or not? I borrowed two big, elderly cases from a friend as I thought they might be useful for storage when I got there, and someone else had said that two cases weighing about the same were easier to manage than one whacking big one. I then added a red rucksack and a soft handbag with a long strap. I could walk comfortably holding all these things - a case in each hand and the other two hung front and rear.

4

Jen suggested I take plenty of clothes and undies because everyone in India is about half my size - I am a bulky size 18. She also thought that I should stock up on whatever my survival is dependent upon - ciggies? booze? Prozak? If I needed any of these three - which I didn't - she told me they would have to be consumed in strictest secrecy because a high standard of propriety is expected of Volunteers in India. (Jen always hid up to smoke her cigarettes).

My list for the actual journey - (how I *love* lists) was cut down to:

Passport, small change, notes, visa card, comb, tissues, watch and alarm clock, book, pen, pad, ticket, chapped lipstick, toothpaste and brush, shampoo, calculator, specs, scissors, camera, address book, towel, slippers, keys, photos, Walkman, dictionary and blotting paper for drying flowers.

I had read Vikram Seth's A Suitable Boy and hoped that India would be something like this book. Would it come up to my expectations in the areas of mysticism, romances, philosophy, and religion? I started to collect paperbacks from second-hand shops and tried to get a balance of books of 'Indian' facts and figures and travellers' experiences but included lots more in the 'escapist' category.

I bought an enormous plastic red torch and exchanged my camera for a slightly better one. I tried very hard to assemble a first aid/medical kit but I have been so boringly fit all my life that I couldn't get excited about the weird potions and remedies that other people warned me to take! They recommended stuff to stop you having diarrhoea and then stuff to make you 'go' again and I decided to forget all that. I did pack Elastoplasts and Aspirin because somehow people always ask me if I have any of those things secreted about my person, wherever I go, especially since I have become a grandma! I searched for some stuff to 'super-glue' my capped teeth back in with, to no avail. These two front teeth have a habit of falling out if I am excited or drunk, but

I decided to try not to be either of those things. The sight of my grin when they fell out at a wedding and again at an anniversary party, has met with such hilarity, I think people think it is my Party Piece. (Writing this I have just wondered if champagne has a bad affect on the teeth glue!)

The authorities don't allow you to take Indian currency into India but I accepted the request by the Minister of the Unitarian Church, in Ipswich to buy some rupees from him that he wanted to 'get rid of'. Someone had donated rupees to his Church and I happily paid him pounds in exchange, only worrying about using his Church like the money lenders in the Bible. He didn't seem to worry though and I happily hid these scruffy old notes in piles of luggage. They would be useful for the taxi from the airport to the hotel in Madras, when I wouldn't want to be searching for a Bank. I was to be paid in rupees at the Orphanage - at the same rate as the carers - and Jen was sure I would find the amount paid more than adequate for a normal life.

The night before my Saturday flight, I met my ex-husband Bob and son Leigh in my local, The Greyhound, to say goodbye. We consumed a moderate amount of their wonderful beer with some friends and said goodbye, *without tears*. This I will never understand because I am usually the soggiest person in these circumstances and yet I felt euphoric, calm and happy. When my "most special" men went off to their respective homes, I went with a couple of friends to try out another Ipswich Indian restaurant before leaving for the *real thing* in the morning.

I declined various offers to run me to the airport because it is three hours from Ipswich by road and I couldn't bear the thought of people giving up what is virtually all day, to run me there. So I got the train and then the Underground and, despite the weight of the luggage, I had to stop myself skipping up the ramp to Terminal Four. Airports to me, are the 'Most Exciting Place to Be' in the whole world. I clutched my rucksack and handbag, after delivering the big luggage, and revelled in people-gazing. I was too enthralled with a couple of Italian-looking sweet-hearts, and a stubble-chinned, swarthy father with a tiny, blonde baby, to bend the ear of my nearest neighbour about my own adventure, which is usually my way. The televised flight times gave me a thrill - seeing my own destination - and such an exotic one - but I tried desperately to look 'cool' and not give away my feeling that I might *burst* if they didn't let us get going soon. In trying to achieve this 'cool' image in the train station at Amsterdam, last year, I stood leaning backwards against a wall, letting it take the weight of my rucksack, left the spoon in the paper cup of coffee, (as I had seen the Dutch do), and surveyed the waiting passengers with that aloof and haughty expression that seasoned travellers have. Then I realised the train pulling out was mine.

I expect the flight to India was routine and uneventful for everyone else but I was seething with excitement and loved every minute of the hours and hours of reading and eating and drinking. I *loved* the plastic curry and the plastic roll and all those little old bits and pieces of salt and sugar and plastic cutlery that won't come out of the packets and which everyone moans about. I scooped them into my rucksack for later distribution at the Orphanage. I wished we could all get out at Amsterdam for a walk around - I *love* Dutch people and Holland. There was a bit of a queue for the in-flight loo before we landed in Amsterdam, en route for Madras, but I wanted to say, "Don't wee over Holland". (Perhaps there is a more sophisticated system in 'planes, these days and the loos don't empty into the air now?)

The lovely gin and tonic brought by a friendly air hostess - they aren't snooty these days I noticed - sent me straight into a long delicious sleep. I wonder why drinks are *so* nice on a flight - even the fresh, salted peanuts seem extra fresh and salty when you are flying. The man next to me had divergent eyes and rather sparse teeth but he said he loved my British accent and thought I talked like Lady Diana so I enjoyed our intermittent chats - he slept quite a lot. He also kept nice and quiet while we landed and I could gulp and goggle out of the window and thoroughly enjoy landing *in India*!

CHAPTER TWO

A night in Madras, and on to Podenur, my new Indian home.

I flew from London to Madras to spend my first night in India. Jen had recommended the Broadlands Hotel as the best place for newcomers. She had explained that since it is for 'Foreigners Only' - you don't feel overwhelmed by the sheer numbers of Indian people, and can swap experiences and collect tips from the other Europeans that fill the small hotel.

An ebullient taxi driver had talked all the way from Madras airport to the hotel, in good English, about his opinion of our loose morals. I can't tell you about the route from the airport because he went on and on about how he knows that Englishwomen even sit *astride* motorbikes, which no Indian woman would think of doing and no Indian man would ever condone. I was riveted by his claims and tried desperately to tell him how innocent and lovely we are - and therefore missed the scenery. I didn't realise that I would lose this debate for the whole of the time I was in India.

The travellers in the hotel were young and interesting but all looked a bit pale and tired out. They were keen to know current news from England and some told me their own interesting stories. One particularly friendly Scottish couple described how they ran a telephone Help line for Teenagers in Glasgow, and they were interested to hear about my job as an Education Welfare Officer and about the bullying problems in schools in England. They were

9

the first people in India to benefit from my own Pictures of the Grandchildren, too. I tried a little walk down the road from the hotel but was somewhat embarrassed - not intimidated - by the attention I caused. Everyone came close to me and examined me curiously. I was under such careful scrutiny that I only barely registered the poverty and squalor around. There was rubbish everywhere and malformed children and adults sitting about. I saw some ragged children aggravating a woman sitting on a step and only realised she was blind when another woman shouted at the children and they ran off.

There were no English road signs or directions posted up anywhere, so I was nervous about getting lost and didn't walk far. The air felt damp and hot - like a blanket enveloping you. In the courtyard of the Broadlands Guest House there were some dusty, exotic plants and the rather uneasy looking travellers - all Western - sat about, making desultory conversation, waiting for the water which had been turned off or had run out - I'm not sure which.

The 'wildlife' in my hotel room were assorted cockroaches and non-malarial mosquitoes, two cats, a mouse, three lizards and more ants than I have ever seen in my life. They shared the breakfast delivered to my room in the early morning - a warm omelette wrapped in newspaper and tied with string, and a very evil-looking green flask of surprisingly good coffee. I didn't know then that the uneasy sleep here was as good as I would get in India in spite of my subsequent superior accommodation.

The next day I had to take a short flight from Madras to Coimbatoire. I was in that dream-like state where you know the adventure is really happening. This was not the dream I had had for weeks, this was IT. Coimbatore airport was small and friendly and I quickly spotted a small group of people watching out for friends. My plane had arrived at about eleven in the morning when there were comparatively few other people about. A smiling, slim, thirty-ish woman shook hands formally and somewhat nervously I thought, and told me her name was Sunbeam. Amazingly - she is such a tiny, shy girl - I learned she was in complete charge of the Families for Children Orphanage. I was to be constantly full of admiration of her capable, calm control of staff and children alike. We went to a waiting car with my luggage and I met Mani, the driver with whom I would also develop a valuable working partnership. The route from Coimbatore to my destination -the village of Podenur - was arid and treeless and there were many unfinished buildings, thatched homes with earth floors, and fields and fields of sugar cane on either side of the pot-holed road. There wasn't much traffic but what there was - motorcycles and cows mostly - seemed to be all over the road, and we wove in and out in a rather alarming way. We didn't talk very much - they were shy and I was avid to see the scenery on the twenty-minute drive to the Orphanage. Sunbeam told me she had a five-year-old daughter, called Sunshine (!) and I showed her the Granny Pictures from England which were already becoming somewhat thumbed. Sunbeam told me her husband was a Pharmacist in Podanur.

I never believed that the smiling boys in the photographs in the Ipswich Church would become my neighbours and friends, but it was amazingly simple and within a couple of months I was *there* - sweating gently in 30 odd degrees of heat and incredible humidity. My fingers and toes were swollen like baguettes from the flight and didn't reduce for weeks, but I was otherwise fit and so happy to be there because it was clear from day one that it would be fun helping the children individually for the year, without having the responsibility of the practical running of the Orphanage.

I had been asked to generally advise the staff and to particularly befriend the 179 fit boys and 35 physically or mentally disadvantaged boys - called the Special Boys - who lived there. After their initial shyness and then curiosity, the children welcomed - even worshipped - me, and fought

11

to hold my hand or carry my hat. The staff were mostly salaried workers who had been there for many years and were used to Volunteer Western workers sharing the joys and tribulations of the project, which was started in 1978. However, they had never had a Volunteer to stay as long as a year, or anyone staying on their own, or anyone of my great age. They made me feel very welcome though.

CHAPTER THREE

Renamed 'Mummy' I meet my new friends and neighbours

On arrival at the village we looked at five units in the Orphanage where the girls, the babies, the boys, the 'special' boys and 'special' girls lived. We called at a large office building, attached to the girls' quarters, where Sunbeam introduced me to two Social Workers, Raji - a beautiful woman of about thirty years - and Ghandi, a smiley man of 28 or so. There were also two men called Mr. Suami, an accountant, and his brother whose name I didn't catch, who was a Clerk. They made me very welcome in a shy way.

Sunbeam and staff

Sunbeam also introduced me to many women working at the orphanage with easy to remember names like Josephine, Celine, Gracie or Enid. They all cared for the children in different ways and had known many Volunteers from the West but still everyone *stared* at me. I felt very self-conscious about this and hoped it was just because it was early days. Even in the street, people came up to me and examined every bit of me - it was quite unnerving.

I was delighted to find a portable typewriter in my new home. An English Volunteer called Bert in the dim and distant past had left it and I thanked him daily for his gift because typing is like talking to a friend for me and I was the only Westerner living in the village. I loved it particularly because it was a *manual* machine and I didn't have to stop when the electricity failed, which it did quite frequently. If I could bear the heat without the fan going, and if it wasn't already dark, I could keep on happily typing. It had the word Volunteer very clearly scratched and painted into its carriage and I learned that this was the reason it was given to me. Apparently if it had not been so 'personalised' it would have disappeared. I typed letters to everyone I knew and that meant I had a whole year of letters *back* from England, which were *so* welcome.

My home was a sort of shed, comprising large sitting room, small bedroom, kitchen, bathroom and a sort of second bedroom, which was windowless and dark, but useful for storage of my suitcases and a rack which I rigged up for keeping my clothes aired. It was all a bit stark but I enjoyed planning how I could improve it and make it 'mine'. The kitchen had stable doors and there were permanent big smiles beaming over the closed bottom half. They were visitors from the Special Boys unit next door. On the same side as these doors, the living room had glass-less windows with ornamental grids, which overlooked a dusty square. There was a big antique bed with an incredibly hard mattress in the bedroom, and another antique piece - a chaise-longue - graced the sitting room. Jen picked these treasures in a shop in Coimbatore that sounded wonderful. (I wouldn't dare go there because if these pieces were anything to go by, I knew I would want *everything* and not be able to get them home.) There was a rickety water tank on a shaky-looking building opposite my house and a small hut next door to it. An elderly man, called Antony, lived in this hut which didn't appear big enough for even a single bed! His wife had apparently thrown him out of his own home, and the Orphanage people had taken pity on him. He had been a worker in the Orphanage for many years but was now too old to be much help, and they allowed him to live in this tiny hut.

On the other side of the square was a boundary fence between it and a small road leading to a housing area. There were a couple of banana trees and two or three coconut trees. I immediately had to take photos of the flowers that preceded the bananas - they were *weird* - in colour and in shape. Really dramatic and exotic. There were also several mango trees, which I had never seen before.

The boys from Boys House and from the unit next door visited this compound, constantly, and I got to know them all eventually, but how I *wished* I could remember their names because they absolutely loved it if I did. They didn't all *look* the same, of course- they ranged from nose runny, scabied, and patchy bald, to big brown eyed and adorable. They all called me Mummy, which was apparently not the maternal Mummy, but a respectful name. Even *old* Indian men and women called me this which took a bit of getting used to at first. It wasn't surprising I couldn't remember their names because they were mostly combinations of the same names - like Mukesh Kumar and Kumar Mukesh or Shanmurgan Mukesh. If they had told me they were just Shanmurgan, or even better, Enid, Josephine or Cyril, I could have remembered them, but of course not many of them had English names. There was one particularly lovely little boy called Cedric. The sticky labels I bought to write their names on, and stick on their shirts to help me, didn't work

15

A drawing competition entry entitled 'Our Garden'

at all. They fell off before I could memorise any of them. However, they all loved wearing them and little Cedric had his label stuck on his bare tum for a day. I couldn't tell Abdul Kumar from Kumar Abdul all the time I was there. The only Tamil (the language spoken by people in the Tamil Nadu region) I learned in desperation, at first, was 'Karee Mucki' - 'wipe your nose'. Oh, and I remembered a few of the plants and flowers because the boys showed me with such pride around their garden. They wanted my help in improving the garden and the plants certainly needed my help. (Pantomiming an explanation of 'compost' was a bit of a challenge). They just loved me to be *interested* in whatever project they had in hand at the time. I was certainly interested in their meals - I saw the biggest Veggie Biriani you have ever seen in your life, which was demolished in minutes. It was cooked in a huge pot over an open fire and

16

there were over a hundred boys sitting so quietly and tucking in using their hands, without cutlery. They then each washed their own plate, and went off to play. There were no pushing or shoving - just rows of smiley faces.

From day one, they loved coming to see me in my house, and greatly admired my Good Luck and Bon Voyage cards, which I hung on the wires that supported the mosquito net. They were curious about my bed, made up with the white sheets and duvet cover bought out on Jen's advice. What with my long, cotton nightie and all this white bed linen, I felt that *Out of Africa* had nothing on me. Every night I leapt into bed with a torch to find the *World Service* on the radio, or reached for a paperback, a bottle of moisturiser and the travel clock, all of which ensured a blissful end to the day.

The fan in my room at the orphanage was a welcome wonder. The one at the Broadlands Hotel in Madras sounded as if it might come down and cut my head off, but those in my house were lovely. I couldn't think for a long time what the sound reminded me of but in the middle of one very hot night I realised it sounded like the sea! I woke thinking I was in Castlerock, in the north of Ireland, with the waves crashing and receding, only to discover that it was the noise of this fan. I missed it terribly - the noise and the cooling relief - when the electricity failed- which it did frequently. Even so, *bed* was a haven of delight throughout my stay in India - even though I didn't ever *sleep* very much. It was a pleasure, even on the nights when the temple bells and/or electioneering Tannoys kept me awake *all* night.

A shower would perhaps have improved my chance of sleeping better in my new home, but although there *was* running water in my house, it was only from a low down tap into a bucket in the 'bathroom', at first. A shower had been promised and the staff were apologetic that it would only be *cold* water. I was sure that wouldn't matter here - the temperature was incredibly high. It helped that the water was hot all the time when it came to house cleaning but my 'help in the house' people returned the floor cloths that were provided for floor cleaning - *washed and ironed* - and never used them again. They occasionally swept the dust up in the air and the floors mostly remained gritty and unwashed. An unusually big (for India) woman cleaned my apartment twice a week but I tried all the time to persuade her and another man that came, not to keep *sweeping* the red dust up in the air both inside and out of the house. Sweeping is an important job in India and Sweeper is a recognised title and an unusually vigorous activity, unfortunately. I often demonstrated the advantage of wet floor cloths to my big Indian Mrs. Mop, but she never understood me, I enjoyed sharing my Sainsbury's Punjana tea bags from home with her. To my huge surprise, tea wasn't half so popular here as in England and I am a tea-a-holic so it was lucky that I had taken my own supplies. Her pleasure in sipping it 'English-style' with me, was lovely, but she was just being sociable - their way of drinking tea is completely different - no milk and in small glasses. I was so pleased my huge Limoges teacup and saucer withstood the journey as I never think tea is as good as when it is properly made in a teapot and poured into a thin china cup. She and I mimed and smiled our way to understanding each other without the benefit of lessons but I soon graduated to talking like Ronnie Corbett 'doing' Indian.

During the first weeks I was definitely a Brit. Abroad - shouting clearly. Since the Indians seemed to want me to teach English to all ages, I knew I would have to re think my strategy. One morning I was going through parts of the body with the little boys, pointing like mad and shouting, "What is this?" at my hair, nose, mouth etc. to demonstrate the word. However, when I pointed at THEIR hair, and said, "What is this?" They all chanted "What is this?"

Even without English they all quickly knew what was needed for one of the first new projects, which was a Weekly Drawing Competition. They were woefully short of paper and crayons but we scratched together enough to compete for three prizes each week and they loved it. One week we tried to draw the Best Flower, the next week, the Best Drawing of Your Friend, and so on. They were all only used to copying other pictures and found free style a new and worrying concept. The results were funny and surprisingly good, though. The prizes were balloons, pens, sweets, and sometimes baseball caps if I could find them in town. I carried nearly two hundred entries from their quarters to my room each week and found four or five that had written their names correctly and who had actually drawn the subject suggested. I then asked any visitor to my house, which of them should receive the prizes. The boys loved it if I could engage someone special to present their prizes and were so enthusiastic in their applause for each other that it was a very happy event in the week.

Some Canadian visitors came to the orphanage just after my arrival and were splendid judges for the Drawing Competition. They ran the Orphanage from Canada and were very interested in my reactions to life in India, and in my intentions and plans for the future year. Two of the visitors looked and spoke like Katherine Hepburn and Spencer Tracey. She was Sandra Simpson, Director of FFC, and he was Dr. Michael Allen, a consultant paediatrician and good friend of Sandra and FFC. I fell in love with him immediately.

There was also a shy girl of Japanese origin, who was nervous about keeping healthy. I never saw her when she wasn't clutching a bottle of bought water and she told me she would never 'eat out' in India. She worked voluntarily in the office in Canada, every Saturday, and this was her first visit to India, too. They were all very friendly and happy - they were the first Canadians I had ever met and I found them just like the Americans I had known in East Anglia. Though they all loved being there, and were obviously very interested in all that was going on, they were very nervous about the hygiene aspect of life in India. They advised me not to touch door handles or banisters or taps in town, and not to eat anything unpeeled or uncooked and gave the warning that I was bound to be ill from time to time, if I stayed more than a few days.

Sandra made it very obvious that she didn't value Volunteers as much as Jen does, but I was so impressed - awe-struck even - by what she had achieved here, that I tried not to mind her disinterest in me. She told me she was initially sure there was a misprint in my C.V. because she hadn't had an offer from a *56-year-old granny* before. She also later reiterated her fears that Volunteers meant complications because of emotional involvement with the Indian men-folk but when I had promised not to fall in love with anyone, she relented and took me on. I expect it was Jen's assertion that I was unlikely to disturb the emotions of either the teenage boys or the elderly staff and that they were far more likely to accept my 'mother' role that had swayed her in the end. I remember coming home from the exhibition in the Ipswich Church and telephoning to ask if they wanted a Volunteer at this time. Jen's husband, Larry, happened to answer the 'phone that day and he told me that they weren't taking on Volunteers any more, because, "Volunteers get romantically involved with the young Indians, upset the old Indians, and have to come home before they have done any work!" I explained that I was an Old English volunteer, and unlikely to upset any Old Indians, so could I be considered? Larry thought perhaps I could and Jen duly approved me.

Sandra's relative coolness contrasted dramatically with the Indian staff, whom I found 'mannerly'. A Scotsman used this word in conversation at the airport, and he was right - they are gracious somehow. Oddly enough, Harry used the same word when he was describing how *he* found the natives to be. Harry was a Dutch/Canadian who was the fourth member of the Canadian party. He had been a benefactor for years and came on 'holiday' from his dairy farm to do practical work wherever he could in the Orphanage. This time he also meant to decide where to spend some more of his hard-earned money in India. He was a big, rosy-faced man, who preferred working with his hands to anything else. His farm in Canada sounded wonderful and though his wife has no interest in travel, (only fund-raising), his sister-in law, Audrey, was coming over soon to see the Orphanage because she is a great fundraiser, too.

Harry was staying for bed and breakfast with some Indians up the road, but the remainder of the Canadian party were in Sandra's 'flat' nearby. They all came for the occasional meal with me and told me the history of Families For Children, and the personalities here. I made 'scratch' meals from odds and ends that had been delivered for me, but gained points for making them hot bananas and honey sauce, even though we had no cream or ice-cream to perfect the dish! They loved 'English' cauliflower cheese, too. They all crammed into my accommodation, which was a single storey extension to the Special Boys Section, and it was fun having company.

Sunbeam invited me to go to buy "wessels", as she put it, to enable me to cook in my little kitchen. I had come to India equipped with tea bags, coffee and my cafetiére. When the cafetiére slipped from my hand and smashed on the tiled kitchen floor, I was very sad. I even searched for the Homeopathic Rescue Remedy for Emergencies (another going-away present which the donor promised would calm me in these sort of crises) until I remembered passing it on to a pregnant friend before I left home. Indians don't appear to drink much coffee, either, so I wasn't optimistic about finding another cafetiére. When they did drink tea or coffee, they had glasses or tiny cups of it with warm evaporated milk, which I managed to avoid most of the time.

When Sunbeam and I went to town to buy a kettle and teapot, we found the stainless steel 'wessels' being sold by the kilo in the road. They all came from the steelworks, which is up the road from the Orphanage. We bought saucepans, a kettle, dishes, and enough jugs to run a hotel kitchen. All these were carefully weighed, on a balance scale, in the gutter.

The people in the Orphanage Office had kindly given me their own luminous green 'fridge which had red hearts stuck all over it but it only worked if you jammed a rock in the socket with the electric plug. Harry, who is so like my ex-husband Bob in that he 'waved a wand' over problems in my house whenever I mentioned them, invented this ingenious repair job. I enjoyed our discussions on how to tackle these jobs and I missed Bob most at these times. I also looked forward to his letters very much.

My next dependency after tea was POST from home. I found the Post Office, the place for sending faxes, and a telephone, which would receive and send calls to England. When the first post arrived for me from England, I was over the moon but I realised early on that I was not capable of speaking on the 'phone to anyone at home. The gulping and shuddering sobs wouldn't have convinced anyone that I was enjoying India, but I just couldn't speak when I heard their voices. I failed the Intrepid Traveller Test on receipt of the first post, too, and was *awash* for half an hour, because the letter from Jane, my daughter, included photographs of my grandchildren, Holly and William. I had managed *not* to say goodbye to Holly and William by pretending that I would see them all again before I left. This worked well and I even spoke on the telephone up until the end, without crying, by saying I would speak to them again before I left. The heavy, miserable feelings I sometimes experienced - in the middle of the night particularly - about leaving *people* - were more about leaving Holly and William than anyone. If I tried to analyse these feelings - which I do all the time about everything - I thought it was because *they* love *me* so much. I suspect that everyone else is a bit fed up with having me about for years and they have certainly all heard my stories twice and told me so, and so I didn't think that they would miss me. I know that if the children lived round the corner from me, I would not be able to leave them. I see them so rarely that I have come to accept that I am not a *necessary* part of their lives due to the distance apart that we live. Leaving my daughter Jane was hard but she has travelled all over the world as a singer and dancer, and when I told her my plans she just sighed and said, "Oh well, I suppose you will have to go and get it out of your system". This was much as I had said to *her*, a few short years previously when she became a Bluebell Girl and before she became a wife and mother. I think she had more trouble explaining to William and Holly, 3 and 5 years old, about grandma and grandpa now living in separate houses, than she did about grandma going on a journey to foreign parts. She finally hit on the story of the Town Mouse and the Country Mouse and the children were very pleased with this explanation. I often wondered, though, if she herself felt disappointment and unhappiness about me leaving her adorable children, but she always gave me encouragement and support and at least appeared to be happy about both aspects of my new plans.

Of course, leaving my mother and father was horrible - they were 76 and 79 respectively and they love me so much, I think, that *guilt* over-rode my other emotions. However, they have always been very adventurous and curious about other countries and I persuaded them in the end that it was *their* fault I had to go. I couldn't sit still and be a granny and 'knit things', as everyone said I should, and I think that my life had taken this turn as a result of their encouragement to me to travel alone, even when I was very young.

I was touched to hear that when Holly demanded to know how long a year was - before she would see her grandma again - Jane told her it would be when Holly's hair grew to her shoulders. Well, she was seen in the garden, after I'd been gone about a month, shaking her fingers through her hair, in the wind, to make the hair grow quicker. I thought that was lovely. William was averring quite joyfully that his grandma was *An* Indian to anyone who would listen to him at his nursery school.

Bob just reckoned I was *crazy*. This reminded me of his comment - in 1986 or so, when he patted the engine of a BRS lorry that I had borrowed to take stuff to Romania in. On the morning of my departure to the Harwich Ferry he had said - "They must be crazy to lend *you* this!" The Indian adventure was equally crazy in his opinion. He has always maintained that I had to have adventures to feed my ego. I can't really argue with this because I don't honestly know why I feel so excited and pleased when I walk out of the door and into the unknown, but I do. Is it my *ego?* Is your *ego* a place you have to feed? Bob reckoned I was never so happy as when I had notes and lists on my desk at our home, waiting for the next trip, be it family holiday or personal expedition. He enjoyed sharing his feelings about my plans with his son-in-law, my daughter's husband, Steve. *His* comments were all in the range of 'bonkers', 'off her trolley' too. But Steve told me privately that he thought it was a good thing to do, following our separation, - to have a complete change of scene.

Leigh (my 33-year-old son) was as encouraging about my planned trip to India as he had been enthusiastic about my Romanian trip. I think he was a bit envious of that trip, when he helped me load up on the morning of our departure, and presented my co-pilot - his ex-girlfriend - and me - with a couple of Yorkie Bars and a copy of The Sun newspaper in the early morning mist at our home. When a family friend asked Leigh what he thought of his mother's Indian venture he said: "Weeeeell! *I* have cut my hair, bought a suit and got a teaching job" - (all these things had seemed miles away when he was 23 years old), "and when I looked round *she* was off to be a bloody hippie in India!

CHAPTER SIX

Introducing Heather and Nancy

An ex-Volunteer from Canada, called Nancy, came to stay with me in my house in March. I re-erected the mosquito net over the bed where Audrey had earlier slept in my living room. I agonised as to whether I should offer *my* bed to visitors but mine is an antique wonderful bed (even though it does have a coconut shredded shell mattress). I fell into it with such relief at the end of each day, so I was reluctant to be generous with it. However, I made a nice fresh fruit salad for her first supper, and hoped that if the man turned up with the Fresh Flesh he had promised me, I could make a good chicken casserole for her and she wouldn't mind the single bed in the living room. When she arrived I was delighted to find her a look-alike for my daughter, Jane. She was 33 years old, tall and elegant and much travelled. She was relaxed and amusing and had an appreciation of the ironies and eccentricities of Indian life, which it was wonderful to share. She had a week to stay in the Orphanage and then would travel round a bit before going home to her 'high-flying' job in Vancouver. On the first morning we were having breakfast and quietly getting to know each other, when Pointy Ears came to visit her for the third time since her arrival. He remembered her from her first visit. She had just persuaded him to go home when Shanmurgan (17 years old and very 'slow') also arrived to call on Nancy with only his shirt on and the biggest - well you know - morning glory - in evidence. We howled - the tears of laughter squirted across the breakfast table. I had been sitting there, quite relieved really, that Breakfast, chez

25

moi, in a foreign country was being quite successful - good coffee and a decent omelette and, sitting by the window looking at the coconut trees, quite civilised. Shanmurgan certainly changed the tone.

When Nancy 'overdid things' a bit in the sun I persuaded her to take a rest, and enjoyed talking through my own problems and queries with her. I particularly admired her attitude to the staff here and tried to emulate her. She pounded in next door, for instance, and stirred up the ethos and got improvements in no time. She told me I had been much too polite and should be firmer. Nancy seemed to be fairly satisfied with the progress of the Orphanage since her last visit and it was fascinating when hearing the backgrounds of the children and staff, from her. I gained tips and suggestions of how I could improve my own performance - mostly in the Be More Authorative vein. And I loved knowing why some of the children behaved as they did - because of their histories.

Another young woman Volunteer, called Heather, was working in the Orphanage at this time. She was a Mormon, or something similar, and was doing a degree in Child Care in the US. Her visit was sort of Work Experience, and she lived in the nearby town and came into the Baby Room every weekday, on the bus. The Baby Room usually held about ten babies and was situated upstairs from the Boys House. It was therefore light and airy and of course with all these adorable babies in it, it was a lovely place to work or just to visit for a cuddle. Heather came to supper from time to time and of course I invited her to meet Nancy. This was the evening when I most noticed Nancy's sense of humour and her likeness to Jane and I had trouble not giggling with her and offending my other guest.

Heather had perfected the Indian head wobble - a sort of movement from side to side when Indian people talk? Well, Nancy at one point walked past me and muttered, "If she keeps that up, she'll have to have a neck brace!" Heather had certainly entered into the Indian style of doing everything - including eating my chicken casserole and dumplings with her hands. She wore a sari most of the time, too, in spite of her rather hard life commuting to Babies Room from Coimbatore every day. She must've been so *hot* and restricted.

Nancy and I had an unusual day out, early in her visit. We caught several different buses, hanging on the straps with no hope of a seat, for miles and miles, to visit a Girls' Hostel. There were always at least fifty people on the buses, wearing jasmine in their hair and silver and gold saris and jewellery or immaculate nylon (!) shirts. (I couldn't help noticing that Indians do not *perspire* like Britons - they are dry and fragrant in impossibly hot conditions).

We visited this Swedish Home for Fallen Women at the end of a long bus journey. When we reached the Home the Matron, a Swedish lady who had been there for years, somewhat grudgingly showed us around. In halting English, she told us she wanted to go home to Sweden and retire later that year but they couldn't find a replacement for her yet. It was a very *Catholic* Home for homeless girls and women. It was beautifully clean and calm and I couldn't imagine that the residents were as funny and crazy as our children, because the ambience was so feminine and tranquil. We were offered lunch in Matron's apartment and shared a laugh about the dozens of ants that scurried out of the little meringues she produced for dessert. Matron had made her own quarters very beautiful and very 'Swedish' with tapestries and samplers and pale blue and white checks everywhere. She enjoyed our admiration and, though her English wasn't very good, she melted sufficiently to talk about her apprehension at returning to Sweden after all her years in India.

Nancy said the unforgettable bit of the day for her was Matron's face when I pantomimed my question as to what the large hall was used for - perhaps ping-pong? Well, on reflection I suppose I should've known better, given the name over the door: St. Maria Magdalena of the Rosaries, and there *were* rosaries, pictures and Holy ornaments everywhere in this hall. While hashing over the day's events, we agreed that we had kept very calm when Matron rebuked us for arriving to visit her *without warning*. The reason for our visit in the first place was to assure her that we would raise and educate a girl she had sent to live with us, *without any warning*.

We finished that day at my house, eating Fresh Flesh - Chicken Casserole (chicken 'arms' Robert, the Orphanage Bursar, called them) - with Heather. It was after this supper with Heather that she confirmed my fear that I had nits and helped me begin clearing them! There was definitely never a dull moment in India. Heather was the expert on head lice and even 'just happened' to have the special nit comb in her handbag.

I was still using 'If They Could See Me Now' as my signature tune, and Nancy agreed it was also suitable for *her* in India. We broke into it all the time because of the bizarre circumstances that kept cropping up. We often found ourselves laughing out loud because of the ludicrous situations we found ourselves in. One day, for instance, I was strap-hanging on the bus with her and was very inappropriately pressed against a sleeping man - I honestly couldn't help it. We were under a first aid box fixed to the drivers' cabin and framed by fairy lights and I was clutching an unwrapped pair of wonderfully tacky, luminous green underpants with 'Honda' printed on them, which I had bought at a stall at the bus stop (They were a joke present for my son Leigh). I was scratching away at my head, not knowing I had 'company' in my hair at that point. At the same time I was rather desperately conversing with a lady carrying a baby, who was wearing a silver anklet hung with silver balls. She told me what they were called and I hoped to buy some for the pupils in the dancing school that my daughter runs - they are so pretty. All these funny incidents happened in such sweltering heat that you just wanted to laugh all the time.

One day we weren't laughing - Nancy was telling me about her marriage. She had found out that her husband was two timing her after only a year's marriage. He still claimed that he loved her and wanted her back. She cried while relating the saga, and I said how nice she looked when she cried. (I said it for something to say, really, but what *can* you say?) She said, "It is because I have had so much practice".

It seemed that the husband and his family thought she should forgive and forget his indiscretion, but she had come to India to get away and think it over, as well as to look up her friends here. I sympathised with her over-riding disappointment and pessimism about a future with him. They had only been married such a short time, had wonderful jobs, were both young and beautiful, had a lovely home and yet *still* he was carrying on with another girl. Nancy felt that if he could be duplicitous when all the ingredients for a partnership were so good, then there was little hope of a long, happy marriage when they had to face the bad times that are inevitable in anyone's life.

We did a fair amount of analysing marriage, discussing the good and bad aspects of it, and so Nancy was intrigued - and so was I - when I heard from Bob that very day that the doctor had told him his blood pressure was now normal for the first time since we were married. I was pleased, on reflection, to realise how quickly I had sprung to defend marriage as an institution. I described how successful my own had been all the while the children were at home and really for most of the thirty-nine years we had been together. In fact I strongly recommended that Nancy go all out to find another husband - through dating bureau, perhaps - when she returned to Canada. Nancy was such a good listener that I then told her of the somewhat traumatic year of *my* married life before leaving for India.

Our beautiful house in the country had to be sold to enable us to half the proceeds. This meant Bob could live in a cottage deeper in the country and I could buy a town base to 'wander from' and return to. Our last house had been our fifth renovation job over the years and possibly the most beautiful, so it was very painful to leave it. However, having had one sale fall through, I was delighted and relieved, while cutting the acre of grass in the garden one Saturday, when Bob came to the door and shouted, "We've Sold!". The solicitor had telephoned to say this sale was secured and our freedom started from there. We immediately opened and drank the champagne that had been waiting in the 'fridge for a year. I started to cook our supper and we opened and drank a bottle of red wine with our supper. I must have drunk most of both these bottles because I don't remember going to bed and when Bob bought the tea in the morning we were jointly disgusted by the sight of my emerald green, grassy and dirty feet. I didn't remember undressing, definitely didn't shower, and couldn't remember writing a Lover List for him. He showed me a piece of paper covered with wobbly writing, listing all the women we knew that I recommended for his next partner.

Bob and I had been creaking on, not adjusting to the 'empty nest' very well, and desperately trying to compromise on a lifestyle for our future. Basically I suppose I wanted to fill the beds in our house with friends and relations and Bob was happiest when we were snowed up alone, and cut off even from the snow plough. We weren't having awful rows, nor had we met more desirable partners, but after our children had left home and we had converted our house from a wreck to a ' des. Country res.', we realised we had no interests in common and our love for each other was diminishing daily. We decided to 'cut and run' while we were still good friends and so I gained *freedom*.

While all this house selling was going on, I learned of the possibility of a year's unpaid leave from my job as an Education Welfare Officer - Truant catcher to you, perhaps? The scheme sounded like legalised truanting for adults and though I had been happily catching truants for fifteen years, I was very gratified when the Local Authority agreed to me having a year off and allowing me to slip back into my same job after a year's absence. This provision is granted to people wishing to 'improve themselves' or 'to help others in the Third World' so I threw myself into finding work overseas to fit my age and experience. This didn't prove too difficult and I enjoyed planning and arranging for the year, while coming to terms with my rather different life as a single woman. I had been 'half of a couple' for ages and it was a bit tricky persuading friends and relatives that there wasn't a 'baddy' in our marriage and they could all relax and treat us in the same way they always had. I understood their confusion about us because more than one person had said we were their role models and were flabbergasted at our new plan.

CHAPTER SEVEN

Physically and Mentally Handicapped Sports Day and another day in Ooty, this time with Nancy.

One Sunday I went to the 'Physically and Mentally Handicapped Sports Day' and was talked into being Prize Giver and speaking on local Radio - only because I was British, of course. About twenty of us - staff and children - went on the specially donated bus and it was dry and dusty and HOT. We met up with hundreds of other children and school staff on a huge, dusty field attached to a large school in the middle of nowhere. We rolled about in the dust, picnicking and awaiting our turn to participate and the children were very excited about it all. Several of our staff felt sick - and were sick - as a result of the bus journey, and some had to lie under the trees, looking as if they might die, during the afternoon.

Amazingly I didn't feel ill from the bus, but was urgently in need of TEA before very long. I went with several of the children and Sophie, a teacher, to try to find tea in the streets outside the grounds of the school. We eventually *did* find a sort of tea-shed and Sophie insisted that she pay for both our glasses of tea-with-evaporated-milk. It was obviously a matter of pride to her, to be able to treat me, so I accepted graciously. We then talked, again, about her need for a sponsor for her sick elderly sister who she cares for at home. She hoped that I could find a kind person to send regular money, in the way that people send it for the children in the Orphanage. I was intrigued to hear her accidentally let slip the fact that she had tried to get my 'gold' necklace melted down for money. I had sent home to ask my mum to send out this 'gold' chain that I wanted to give to Sophie. She had told me so often how she admired English 'gold' because black marks didn't appear on your skin when you wore it. I *had* wondered why I had never seen her wearing it - can't think what sort of mess arrived when the jeweller tried to melt it, because it certainly wasn't gold!

After our tea party we started to walk back to the sports field and met a seven-year old, genius pupil from the school, who stopped us to ask if he could talk English *at* me? I said yes and got ready for the usual halting questions about how I found Indian cuisine, *etc.* but to my amazement he launched into an explanation of the workings of some *pyramids* built in the grounds of his school. He towed us all for miles around the sports field and to the rear of the main school and there they were. Looking incongruously Egyptian, they were billed outside as Good for Mental Constipation. The little boy invited some of us in and we went down about fifty uneven and poorly lit steps, into pitch darkness. In loud whispers he suggested we sit on the floor and meditate on our personal health for five minutes. I couldn't put my mind to meditate on anything except how I was going to get about twelve of our mentally handicapped children *out* of the pyramid. When we did emerge, Genius Boy asked if we would like to see the swimming pool and took us to *see* the most beautiful, Hollywood style, swimming pool with *no* people in it. It was glittering and gleaming in the mid-day sun and was like a mirage in a desert. Then he said I couldn't use it because I was a woman. It is the only one in Tamil Nadu but women aren't allowed to use it.

I immediately made elaborate mental plans for bringing our children to learn to swim in it, but how to get an invitation was a problem. After writing a begging letter to

Genius Boy's Head teacher on the only available paper - the back of a Pepsi label - I realised that our boys and girls had never been in water that deep before - or even in a bath - so perhaps it wasn't such a good idea.

An orange-clad 'muse' had engaged me in conversation on the field earlier and had been talking to the staff while we were away from the dusty field. He apparently told one of the other Orphanage helpers that he found me "incredibly and unusually active for such an elderly woman." *He* was elderly, and only wore an orange skirt, had a grey bun, a grey beard down to his bare navel, and a whacking great bead necklace. He recommended that I should speak on the local radio to gain donations for the Orphanage from the listeners. I agreed to do this, if he would like to formally write to Sandra in Canada to get permission. I would like to have talked to him more about his philosophy of life, but the children got fed up waiting for me to stop talking.

Another interesting person I met was a veteran pole-vaulter. She was extremely beautiful, about sixty years old,

Saravanen

and had just represented India, abroad, in an important World event, that I can't remember the name of. She was a doctor of homeopathic medicine, as was her husband, and she gave me her card to visit and 'talk about things' so I thought I might try to find her again one day because she was so vital and interesting.

The sports events themselves were emotionally choking all day. There were callipers flashing in the running races and crawling races for those with 'impaired mobility' - like no legs at all. There was deaf and dumb parcel passing with signing to stop the parcel and Blind Man's Buff with no blindfolds needed that day. I didn't hear anyone cry or lose his or her temper all day. We rolled about in about six inches of dust from 7 a.m. to 7.30 p.m. and the 'incredibly active woman' was a bit of a disaster area by 8 pm I can tell you.

On the bus going home someone told me that one hundred thousand people would be watching the Test Match at the Eden Gardens, Calcutta, that night. I knew everyone at the Orphanage would be interested and was therefore dismayed to learn that Jamal, Boys' supervisor, had decreed that TV would *not* be allowed that evening - punishment for some previous misbehaviour. I wished I could 'interfere' and get them a reprieve, but didn't think I had better.

Nancy and I had an incredible day in Ooty. When I say incredible - it took us all the following day, to get over it. I had been there before but by car and so was more than pleased for an excuse to go again so that I could experience the famous, small-gauge railway. There, standing in the station was this lovely, small, steam driven train, with about twenty wooden, well-painted carriages. There were oval, glazed windows in the doors, no corridor but open seating for about twenty in each carriage. The journey took four and half-hours to Ooty, through misty blue/green tea plantations and generally spectacular scenery. It cost less than £1. We were told that it was going to be 'dieselised' next year so when we passed over gorges on bridges that were just the size of the rail tracks and we could see the shadow of the train and the *steam* from the train, in the bottom of the gorge, it was very exciting. The passengers were all Indians in holiday mood. We saw only three Western tourists all day, and *we* stared at *them* in just the same way as the Indians stared at us. We looked *so* white, out there - and *ill and jaded,* really.

The signs that we saw written up in the station in Coimbatore were a delight even before we arrived in Ooty:

Rose Pepsi (honestly, we tasted it and found it to be flavoured with roses)

Teena Tailors

A firm of financial advisers who vowed that they were 'Hypothecated to the Community District Central Co-operative Bank '

Do Not Touch Unclaimed Toys or Transistors Found in Public Places - Inform the Matter to the Railway or public Official as per possible

Do Not enter into the Platform to see of your friends or relatives

Please watch the movements of strangers and their activities - available information suitably rewarded!

And how about:

Indian Railways
Indian Pride
By Cleanliness
We do Abide!

By the track we saw monkeys, acacia, bougainvillaea, Old Man's Beard, Yucca, Bananas, Buddleia 'forests', and salvias that grew several feet tall instead of inches. We travelled in long tunnels through the mountains and it was funny to see just the whites of the Indians' eyes in the

36

darkness. Because the track wound round mountains it was spectacular looking ahead, leaning out of the windows, and seeing the steam coming from the engine and the smiling driver waving backwards out of his carriage to us.

We hired a taxi for the afternoon for one pound and visited the Botanical gardens - second visit for me to see this well-publicised park, which still had only bedraggled plants on show. However, Nancy loved the Victorian, English styled buildings and landscaped parkland, and we stood on the highest point in Tamil Nadu and smelled beautiful fresh air for the first time in a month. We could see the pollution belt below us - gosh, it's serious there. There's a sort of kerosene/smoke/garbage blanket over everything below a certain altitude.

A handsome New Zealand chap stopped to talk to us - we were the only white people in Ooty I think - and fell in love with Nancy. It was a pity it was the end of the day because I am sure he would have loved to have spent the day with us - well anyway with Nancy.

Ooty was one of the hill stations where the military wives and children went for a holiday in the old days during the hot seasons. They had large houses and estates called Fernhill or Runnymeade or Glendale, and I saw a road called Lloyds Avenue and a house called Bank House, names of houses and places I had lived in, in the forties and fifties, in Ipswich. Ooty was pretty densely packed with people and catered for tourists in that many of the market stalls had colourful luggage, leather goods and luminous underpants etc. As in other towns and villages, I saw very few people smoking cigarettes and I didn't see anyone drinking alcohol all day. I saw a Gold Flake, yellow, cigarette packet thrown away, which I hadn't seen for years - do we still have that brand in England?

Nancy bought leather belts as presents for all the boys in Special Care. They were so delighted in the morning when we helped them put them on and she couldn't have chosen a better present. However, when we took them into their

37

house, the boys were so excited and aroused by having two women helping them put them on, that we didn't know whether to fix them with the buckle in front or behind the 'frontal problem'.

After a bit more shopping - eucalyptus oil and every other known oil was Ooty's speciality - we got the bus home. This sounds all right but in fact it wasn't. It was five hours of jolting, sickeningly smelly, boiling hot journey with evil-looking men (that weren't, of course), fifteen hairpin bends (helpfully numbered), dark streets and dangerous, unlit traffic.

Nancy vowed that I was using her as an experiment in stamina and she was still looking green and poorly, 24 hours later (No stamina, these youngsters, I thought). However, she did say that I only got on her nerves once, all day, and that was when I enquired during the miserable night drive if she, or I, would cook our supper when we got home?

The only laugh we had managed on the Grisly Bus Journey was about the First Aid Box. They usually have them at the front of the bus and they have flashing lights like Christmas decorations and a big, important FIRST AID written on them in English - which most of the people of Tamil Nadu can't read anyway.

Well this bus had a notice saying 'F.A.' on a glass-fronted box showing it to have F.A. inside!

The journey was so grisly that Nancy and I discussed what we would do in the event of an accident and promised each other that we would not let anyone else treat us. I was glad to know that she had got an 'A' in Needlework for if she had to sew me up, and she seemed pleased to know that my husband once taught me mouth-to-mouth resuscitation. I passed some time on the journey recollecting for Nancy the reason he had taught me: I had the sad job of calling the police and ambulance to a boy that had died from electrocution when his tip-up lorry had struck live wires in Suffolk one morning. I was the first on the scene and was worried that I had not known how to do mouth-to-mouth resuscitation, even though it would have been useless to do it in that instance. A few mornings afterwards, I hastily demanded a demonstration from Bob before I left for work - "just in case" I ever had the need again. I have to admit the lesson made me *very late* for wor.

On our return life in the orphanage got back to normal. The food situation when I had visitors was stretching my cooking skills, even though by then Nancy had reassured me that I 'needn't go to any trouble' for *her*. One day nine papayas, seven eggs, one small pineapple, a half a kilo of peas and some elderly string beans were delivered!

I learned such a lot about working in the Orphanage from Nancy. She didn't *let go* of any problems - however "nozzious" - no one says nauseous like Canadians do they? She attacked all the shortcomings of the staff without worrying about offending them and I tried to copy her firm, pleasant style. I had felt very hesitant in the field of staff management and caring for disabled people. Nancy had no hesitation in, for instance, cancelling the use of a stiff old bristly brush that the staff were using to clean the boys in the washroom and it was never seen again. I had been psyching up to 'steal' it for ages.

I loved having Nancy there for company but I wrote home to put English friends off coming here for their holidays with me. Life in the Orphanage, and the village, was such a mixture of ghastliness and joy that I know it would not have suited many people. It is very difficult to explain how, even though it was filthy dirty everywhere, with people spitting and worse and rubbish up to your armpits in the streets, it was still a wonderful experience to live there. It certainly wasn't many people's idea of a holiday resort, though, and I felt you needed to *live* the Indian experience for several weeks to fully appreciate it.

The day that Nancy departed will perhaps explain how odd it is here, with lovely 'happenings' alleviating the horrible things. I was crying away in the back of the motorised pram called an auto-car, because I had seen

Nancy off at the airport and didn't think I'd ever see her again. The driver - smiley Anthony Williams Jackson - kept turning round to ask why I was howling. Well, I told him to keep driving and not to look at me, but he took me directly to his sister Daisy's house, "because she is good at cheering people up". He also returned my five-rupee note fare, 'Because your purse is empty'. Daisy was a teacher who was having a house built and she told, me I must be Guest of Honour when it is 'inaugurated' in May. She didn't seem at all perturbed at the sight of a washed out, red-eyed foreigner on her doorstep at 6.30 a.m. She made me a cuppa and we had a lovely 'natter' in perfect English, as if I was an old friend of hers.

By 20th March the temperature was 96F degrees and still rising. I was chewed by nits and mosquitoes, still a rather nasty yellow colour in the sun, and probably courting Alzheimers by drinking water boiled in *aloominium* pans - (Nancy's pronunciation), but I wrote home to say that I was Full of Beans and Fit as a Nit. Talking of nits, my nice teacher/neighbour kindly showed me a blown up picture of head lice - which made me feel much better as you can imagine. She said I caught them by letting the boys wear my hat, and I expect she was right.

There was a rich Indian 'benefactor' who always sent gifts to the (female!) Western Volunteers. I had never met him but he lived in a big town nearby and sent 'offerings' to me every now and again. One day's surprise delivery was a huge papaya, about eight chapattis and a pan of soup, which had sweet corn kernels and spices in it. One spoonful of the soup lifted my head off - it was so spicy - but the other things were wonderful.

Food generally was a bit crummy, and I had started daydreaming of a crusty baguette and some sparkly white wine from time to time. Still, who would have thought that a Pepsi from the 'fridge would become as welcome as a G&T - which it was. I boiled drinking water in my pressure cooker but there was a sort of soup left in the bottom when

40

you boiled it, which I didn't like the look of. I investigated an electrical gadget in the shops, which cost about £90 and put the water through ultra violet rays (or something) and it supposedly came out healthy. I thought that sounded like a good idea and determined to get some money from home to buy one.

CHAPTER EIGHT

Illnesses - theirs and mine!

Every now and again I was asked to escort children to the local outpatient clinic in a large hospital. I enjoyed taking them for these appointments because I had an opportunity to really get to know the boys. One day I visited with seventeen-year-old Shanmurgan, and nine-year old Babu. Babu wanted to run away from the orphanage all the time and was allegedly brain-damaged. We had to wait two hours in the Clinic and the other patients waiting in the small cell, which was the waiting room, were very unusual. One was a man chained to a policeman. He was about forty years old, great fun, and talked intelligently in somewhat broken English about his experiences - including growing rhubarb. He offered me his address in case I ever needed it. I couldn't think why the Indian ayahs with me appeared to disprove my new friendship, and she later had grudgingly agreed that the prisoner, "spoke quite nicely". Then she told me that the accompanying policeman had told her that the man was a murderer!

Waiting on the other side of me was a young, voluptuous girl whose family kept pulling at her, and covering her up, and it seemed as if she couldn't stop undressing herself. All this was quite entertaining until the electricity failed and we were plunged into darkness. It got hotter and hotter without the fan and the girl kept stripping off and the murderer went to sleep wearing my hat. They were both eventually summoned to see the same rather disinterested doctors that we saw with our boys later. I had to work quite hard to persuade these superior beings to hear our boys' histories and symptoms, but they lethargically scratched themselves and eventually re-arranged a change of medication for both of them and told us to return in a month. We then waited for the motorised rickshaw, called an auto-car, to get home. We were on a bench with about sixty people staring at us. I was sweating and scratching and holding on to their medical record cards and trying to keep Babu from running off, so I suppose we would have been good entertainment in any waiting room in the world.

After a few days of his revised tablets, Shanmurgan stopped lying about all day covered in flies and even joined in lessons. Babu didn't improve quite so dramatically but the doctor had been quite optimistic about him and had told me to bring him back after a month to report on his progress.

The afternoon of that same day was less dramatic but very pleasant. I painted my bathroom with a lovely tin of yellow paint. The mural-painting-Sam donated a brush and some spirit and I have never achieved such a dramatic transformation as I did in this room. I had to lock myself in and close the windows because so many people wanted to 'help' me and I couldn't be seen in my uncovered state/ decorating gear. There was quite a queue of curious visitors when I finished and they all approved it, "SOOPER MUMMY". I couldn't wait for it to dry so I could use it. The cockroaches must have been 'sore amazed' at the difference in their surroundings. Talking of which, I saw a creature about the size of a baby crocodile, which I thought was a lizard, running up and down a tree near my house. However, there were less attractive creatures about and murdering the bugs became a way of life. I dealt with most of them by lifting them in a duster and throwing them out of the door, but every now and again there was a Very Large One, and these specimens I smashed flat and shovelled under the bed. Some other smaller bugs would come along and have a banquet eating them up. I was dealing with a medium-sized stag-beetle type of bug when I got an amazing phone call from England.

The nearest telephone to my house was five minutes walk down the road, in the Special Girls' Unit Office. It was locked up by so many watchmen, and there were padlocks and grilled windows everywhere, and so it was unusable by me, or any visitor here, or so I thought. However, on this particular Saturday night an ayah from Special Girls came running up, very excited, to say my daughter was calling from England. I sprinted to the Unit and was so surprised and pleased to hear her that I didn't *cry* which is usually my problem with telephone calls, and why I seldom made them. It was wonderful hearing her, but it was a bit like a Chinese meal - you are full up and excited by the content, but half an hour later you wish you had said this or that, and want some *more*. It livened up my Saturday night though and I went back to deal with the stag beetle walking on air.

I have to admit I was sun-stroked one week. It was 100F degrees on my outside thermometer, but I hadn't consciously noticed the difference and had carried on with the Immensely-Popular-Walks-With-Mummy. The result, of course, was that I keeled over. My own temperature was 104 degrees for the first time in my life and I began to think, one night, that I might be like my great-uncle Robert Hamilton McCombe from Northern Ireland, who expired with heat-stroke in Cawnpore, India, in 1931. He was in the Royal Horse Artillery and only in his twenties when he played polo without a helmet, got sunstroke, and died. I was luckier, however, and after four Paracetamol, hundreds of sponging-downs in the hot shower (it didn't 'do' cold) and a bit of a rest, I returned to health and vitality and was definitely a bit wiser.

In India it seems it is the custom to visit anyone who is ill. Can you imagine anything more horrible? Just as you are feeling (and looking) mosquito-bitten, feverish, with cold-sores and nits again, of course, then the most elegant, saried women and dashing, flashing-teethed men, call on you. I told them that in England we keep out of the way of ill friends in case we catch what they've got.

I was a bit mystified as to why these visitors thought I had *boils* when they came to visit me. It seems Robert, the Bursar, thought I told him I had 'boils' when I said I was 'boiling' hot and had spread the news that I needed visiting, because of boils. I learned that these funny misunderstandings often arose because many Indians at the Orphanage were deaf and that is why they often have trouble understanding me or misinterpret what I say. It isn't always that they don't understand English, they just cannot hear properly.

The worst thing that happened, during my 'illness', was one day after tea, when I had battened down the hatches and taken the pills and was creeping off to die quietly, when six people, accompanied by the Watchman, came to pray for me. Honestly. They first of all suggested I led the prayers but I must have given the hint that this was not likely to be a good idea so they proceeded to sing Tamil Healing Music, standing in a ring in the middle of my living room. Well I kept my eyes down and tried not to think of anything particular, so as not to laugh, but then my eyes fell on the man next to me who had only three toes on one foot - beautiful ones but definitely only three.

During the worst night of my affliction I left a drink of purified water on the kitchen table with the Paracetamol. It was all covered up with beaded crocheted covers and left out in case my temperature continued to rise. Well it did, and I staggered in the dark into the kitchen and gulped everything and fell back into bed. In the morning I found the remainder of the drink   full of ants. I'm happy to say I got radiantly well but I wonder how many I swallowed - ugh!

While I had been out of action, a mini-crisis had occurred regarding the burning of the rubbish outside the Special Boys' house. I mollified (I hoped) the ugly, cross neighbour

45

who was complaining vociferously about what had happened. A few weeks previously I had suggested the bin be moved to a spot marginally nearer to this man's house, but between the two buildings, where there was a through draught. I had arranged this because the rubbish was being burned, daily, in the cylinder and the smoke went straight into the Boys' rooms. The irritable neighbour didn't think it should have been moved so I had to do a persuasion job on him - it was nowhere as near to him as it had been to the Boys' Unit and the prevailing wind took it away from both places.

On this same day I also prepared the Orphanage flat for the arrival of the Jen and her sister-in-law, Marlene, which I was looking forward to very much. Meanwhile, at the Boys House, Jamal the Boys' supervisor went off to a wedding with no notice to anyone (which is normal I must admit) and he didn't return until sixteen days later. I suggested to him, on his return, that he should be punished in the way that the boys are punished if they 'bunk off'. They have to kneel in the sand without trousers and with their hands on their head, for ages, and miss their supper. The first time I saw this punishment being used, I was appalled to discover that nice Mary - the woman supervisor at Boys' House - had decided it was appropriate for two boys who had not paid attention in *my* English lesson. I couldn't help thinking of the children I used to try to persuade to return to school in my job at home. I bet this punishment would have achieved regular attendance.

Robert bought me some pellets that you lay on a little machine, which burns for three hours, like incense, and kills all mosquitoes. By the look of my legs it was a bit too late but it might have meant that I wouldn't need the mosquito net which would make sleeping cooler, so I was happy to try them out. The Coconut Collector, who strongly recommended their use, delivered them. He climbed up one of the three coconut trees outside my house and although I was sorry they were going to be harvested because they looked so exotic and tropical, the crunch as they hit the ground made obvious the need to collect them! He halved a big one with an enormous knife, without cutting his arm off, and thrust the knife into the back of his skirt without cutting his buttock off - as far as I could see. While this was happening a Pocahontas lookalike called to say if I shaved my hair off because of the nits, could she have the curls, please?

Around that time I decided to extend the Immensely-Popular-Walks-with-Mummy that the Special Boys were enjoying, to the other boys in Boys House. We went out most days, between their bouts of homework. Apart from their hike to school and back they didn't walk about their village at all and didn't really know their neighbourhood - or meet the neighbours. The route we chose took in a Catholic Church that I had to physically stop the boys running into - they were so keen on seeing the statues and pictures. I always hoped to catch the eye of any of the 'brethren' walking about and wriggle an invitation out of them, so we could go in officially. There was also a slide and a swing surprisingly placed in a remote part of the route, and the nearest thing to a play area I saw in India - which the boys loved to use. They amazed me with their patience - there was no arguing about whose turn it was to go on it and they waited so nicely (I wondered when do they forget this patient attitude, as they grow up, and start elbowing and shoving to get on buses, like their elders?).

There was also a sort of bandstand with seating all round. I used to let them climb and run about on it, at this point of the expedition, but learned later that it was a 'religious' spot for some reason, and should be treated with respect. I didn't have to tell them to be respectful when we came to a strictly guarded house and garden where the presence of the policeman outside struck a chill in their hearts. They always rushed past him fearfully, hanging on to me if they possibly could. They all had a very healthy respect for any military personnel, too.

On our return from the walks, we would pause in the entrance hall of the Boys' House to admire the prize-winning drawings or whatever project was currently displayed. We once pinned their personally created butterflies on to an old sari, to decorate the foyer, and because there were so many of them, they made a fine impression. They made them with the very few colouring pencils and paper that we had there and can you imagine three pairs of scissors between 180 boys?

I thought I'd provide a big wall chart with all the days of the year, on which they could write their birthdays. They didn't all know when their birthdays were but I found most of them in the Office files. I wished I had had some training as a teacher though - I was desperate for ideas on how to entertain them with no materials. One morning's thrill for the little boys waiting to go to school was a biro 'watch' I drew on their lovely chubby brown arms, and they appreciated even my inadequate repertoire of songs.

I had barely finished writing home to say how well I was, when bronchitis struck me for the first time since 1974 and I had to have time off work. It cleared up completely with some pretty pills that I chose from the Pharmacy in the shed next door. I spotted some that had "icillin' written at the end of a word on the label and whatever they were, they did the trick. I don't know if it was a high temperature, or those pills being a bit 'strong' but I definitely hallucinated in the night! On the ceiling I saw goblins and witches pointing with bony fingers from pools of a coloured 'oil on water' effect and when I shifted my gaze to avoid them, there were *more* of these hobgoblins up in the corners of the room. They were sticking their tongues out and grimacing at me which was incredibly disturbing but I must have slept eventually and I had completely recovered from the illness - or the drugs - within a couple of days. It was whilst languishing on my day bed, recuperating, that I sighted my hip bones for the first time since before my children were born thirty years ago.

There seemed to be a lot of illness in the Orphanage at that time and one little boy was sent away to his country relatives with chicken pox. As soon as the diagnosis was made the children and staff were advised by the Orphanage doctor to sleep on beds of neem leaves and eat portions of these same leaves, to prevent infection. Josephine swore by them as a pesticide, too, and waxed very lyrical about the properties of neem *oil* for aching joints, and purification of the air. I can't remember what the tree looked like but I remember seeing it had yellow berries when it was pointed out to me. I hadn't much confidence in this stuff, though, and I put in a bid for an isolation room to be built just inside the gate and about fifty yards from the main building. At that time they just put a sick child in a room within the main block, on a carpet of neem leaves, and expected the others not to go near him. The neem leaves were the only attempt to effect a cure. The infectious children were never given anything to do when they were isolated and had a pretty miserable time in consequence. There was a couple in the 'isolation' room on the day the Birthday chart took off. It was a huge success. I provided a card, a balloon and a small cake from the shop and some of the children cottoned on to sending their own cards to each other. Then we lit a candle, sang The Song, and the birthday boy offered a bite of his cake to me (or someone else if I could get out of eating cream cake at that hour of the morning) before eating the rest himself. The boys who did not know when their birthdays were, asked to have either Christmas Day or my birthday, 2nd May, so there were a great many names squeezed into these sections of the enormous calendar. I was impressed when the Birthday boy on the first morning, remembered his friend who was isolated with chicken pox and sent his cake to him.

At Easter I was called to come to Boys House at 5 a.m. - yes, in the morning a.m. - to help hide eggs. A long time ago a Volunteer started the Egg Hiding for Easter and it had been a huge success ever since. I was so pleased that I hadn't got to *paint* the eggs as well as hide them, that I happily agreed to hide them and it was great fun. Some of the staff stopped up most of the night painting them beautifully, and all the children were SO excited and raced about searching for them. I wished I could tell that Volunteer of the success of his or her idea and how the tradition has been maintained.

CHAPTER NINE

Mariumuthu's visit to the Cinema, a Very Wet Sunday service and visitors from England - Kate and Patrick.

One of the older Special boys, called Marimuthu, was a lovely, thoughtful boy with no proper legs, through poliomyelitis. He was about 20 years old and had been so helpful to me because he spoke more English than most of the boys. I promised him that when an English-language film came to the town, I would take him and his friend Kumar to see it. This happy outing meant enlisting the help of a driver who would be willing to come out in the evening and to lift both boys in and out of the van and into the cinema. Lovely Mani (our driver) agreed to help and I think he was just as excited as the boys about the cinema visit. We set off in high spirits as neither boy had ever been to a cinema or even out at night in the dark for ages. The film selected - for its English - was Speed - which of course turned out to be an American film in which every other word seemed to be f*** or s*** so they didn't learn much of benefit in that respect. However, in all other respects it was eminently suitable because it was all about crashing vehicles and flames, explosions, lifts plunging and similar drama all the way through. They absolutely loved every minute of it. We had Pepsis, crisps (salted *and peppered*), wonderful seats (grotty horrid cinema though) for about £4 for all of us. The boys didn't seem to mind the notice saying 'Please

Do Not Place your Limbs on the Seat in Front' which, as they had no lower limbs, I thought was a bit insensitive. The boys and Mani all agreed it was Soopa Mummy. Mind you, given the hairy journey there and back in the dark, the decibels of the stereo sound, and the content of the film, Mummy deserved all the adoration she got.

The Pharmacist at the orphanage spoke good English but often asked for my help with translations and one day he asked me to translate some <u>German</u> instructions on a packet of tapeworm pills. I took it home to read with my glasses on, but found it to be Arabic writing. This meant I didn't lose face, when I said I couldn't help. I probably would've gone down in his estimation, had it been German, and I failed to decipher it. The Pharmacist argued that it might be Canadian when I told him it wasn't German after all.

The Elim Pentecostal girls invited me to their Sunday evening ordinary Service. I thought the big thunderstorm that erupted just as we should have been setting out, would have put them off calling for me. However, there they were, bedraggled and soaked to the skin and obviously expecting me to go with them. The storm produced a river of water from my house to the house with an upstairs room that was 'Church' for the night. I sat, absolutely drenched, on the only chair in a room full of men and women absolutely absorbed and intensely involved with praising Jesus. They played drums, sang songs, shouted, rolled about on the floor, or prayed silently. There was lightning flashing every few minutes, which lit up the coconut trees outside the iron gridded windows. The sky was navy-blue and there was no light or fan in the room due to a power cut. I feared the candles all over the floor would ignite some of these fervent souls but I guess they were all too wet.

The Minister (a Sri Lankan) suddenly shouted in English: 'Have you found Jesus, Sister?' I looked round to see whom he was talking to, but my friend whispered, "Stand up, Mummy" so I did. He repeated the question and I nodded nervously, just to be friendly. He then offered to translate my reply to the congregation, if I'd like to explain to him *how* I'd found Jesus. I stuttered out an account of my interest in different religions and my appreciation of their invitation (well, that bit was true) and sat down. Then this Minister explained loudly how *he* had been a cigarette-smoking, cricket-playing, loudmouth for years and then - spoiled himself and changed, I wondered? No! Apparently he wanted us join him in fervently thanking Jesus for coming into his life and helping him to give up these sinful things. With his renewed faith he had requested a new <u>W</u>ehicle to replace the one he had had to sell when he went to Dubai to work. The job in Dubai had failed and he had returned to India and missed his motorbike very much. I learned later from a friend in the congregation, that another <u>W</u>ehicle *did* come back into his life.

I had by this time realised that I had lost my door key in the flood on the way to Church. I sat worrying away because my home was an impregnable building when locked. However, at some point the Minister invited people to make their own personal prayers so I fervently prayed that I would find my key. The Lord gave them to someone who had followed us in, and he gave them to me a few minutes later - what about that?

On Good Friday I was invited to another Elim Pentecostal meeting at some unpronounceable but not far-off place. However, Sunbeam declared it would be too hot for me, that day, and she sent two girls to accompany me to a Catholic service up the road instead. I was happy to be redirected because it was fascinating going to all these different religious meetings.

The Hindus seem to have some very colourful customs but the Hindu people I met didn't know enough English to explain them to me. I don't think they are very keen on Christians entering their temples, either. There's a Hindu story about an elephant, called Garnesh, with six arms, that I tried to track down because he is very popular around here, but I had no success. All I gleaned is that he is the Son of Shiva and he can destroy obstacles in your life. A man I

Playground equipment donated by the Mormons

talked to near the Asbestos factory told me that Hinduism
is a personal interpretation of reverence to God, and I saw
that many Indians pray silently in front of garish symbols
in their attempts to get in touch with God. They offer gifts
of rice, incense, flowers and garlands of flower heads - called

poojahs - in the open air shrines, so I suppose that goes on in the temples, too. The married women and young girls all wear jasmine in their hair - every day - but not widows. Another custom is the kum-kum or bindi worn by men and women as a spot on their foreheads. I was often 'anointed' with one of these spots as I left peoples' houses - it was a wish for my *married* happiness.

A Mormon couple - Americans called Joyce and Wesley - came to play with the boys next door every Thursday. They were in their late sixties I would say, but enthusiastic and very energetic. They lived about twenty miles away and came to play ball and other strenuous games, in the most horrendous heat, and never failed to turn up. If I heard the boys laughing outside, it was almost certainly because the Mormons had arrived. There were also two young American men that were 'trainee' Mormons, but they didn't come quite so regularly. When they did come, they spent more time with me than with the boys and I think they liked to have a natter with a mother figure, or someone from the West, rather than playing with the kids. Joyce and Wesley sometimes sat and had a cold drink with me, (Mormons are not allowed tea and coffee) and Wesley once came especially to talk to me about the Mormon faith. He had a very low-key approach in telling me all about it and accepted my arguments quite happily. I never felt worn down by him at all - he was gently informative. Their name is really The Church of Jesus Christ of the Latter Day Saints. It seems that their elders allowed men to have second and third wives at some time in their history - because of the shortage of men - and many sisters had the same husband. They baptise by total immersion and don't believe there is a Hell.

Joyce and Wesley had written to their own children who were active Mormons in America, and told them the situation here. Within a few months a huge amount of dollars arrived to buy play equipment for the children. Their son and daughter had collected the money for the kids and wanted them to buy something that was *fun* and not a basic necessity this time. The equipment was all pretty crudely made but was painted in situ in bright colours. The children were *not* allowed to go on it, at first, until a formal inauguration and thanks session had been arranged. I couldn't believe how they obediently kept off the equipment for ages, even though it was just outside their door. As soon as we had had the official opening, the apparatus was used non-stop by children - and staff - and probably still is being used today. Some of the swings were situated outside my house and one morning - 5.30 a.m. actually - I had to go out and oil a swingboat in desperation because the squeaking was driving me mad. As I poured the oil in, the children stood underneath, either massaging it into their hair like mousse or gel, or drinking it. Never were a few ounces of sunflower oil so beneficial to so many.

I loved Wesley, when the Indian staff asked him to say a few words at the formal Inauguration of the Play Equipment. He started off, speaking quite normally, explaining that it was his *children* that had collected the money for the swings, and not himself. Then his voice started to wobble and he got really emotional and had to stop, and one of the Indians took over the speechifying. Afterwards he was embarrassed about how he'd been affected, and didn't know what to say to *me*. Anyway he was really relieved when I jeered and laughed at him for 'losing it' - and threatened I would write and tell his kids how he'd been. We all ended up laughing *with* him but he'll never know how I *sympathised* with him, in fact, and was awash myself, right through his speech.

Shanthi, the teacher from next door, inspected my kitchen regularly. She couldn't keep away actually, and was fascinated with all my 'things'. She was poking about one day and found some potato crisps that I had put away to savour privately - though I never think they are the same without a pint of bitter. Anyway, they were full of ANTS.

She was most surprised that I didn't want them after this infestation, and happily took them off to share with the boys. Shanthi had terribly cracked, bleeding heels, which seems to be a common complaint here. I was sympathising with her one day, and offered her Vaseline and Socks and the following instructions:

1. Scrape off the dry skin with my English scraper from Boots
2. Smear heels liberally with Vaseline
3. Sleep all night with socks on over the Vaseline.

This always worked for me; even when they had been really bleedy and sore and so, several days later, I enquired how her heels were, following my recommendations. She immediately ran into the little schoolroom and returned with my jar of Vaseline, saying Jesus would not approve of this as it was 'medication' and so she was not allowed to use it and she was just wearing the socks and hoping for improvement.

She then launched into a story about a rat that had been visiting the boys in Boys' House, while they were asleep. I fell about in horror and got them to show me the hole where it was coming in. I then ordered it to be blocked off *tout suite*. However, nothing happened, and Jamal, the supervisor, promised for three weeks that 'he would be doing it that day' - but he never did do it, so I had a tantrum. I flounced off to the building supplies shop and bought the necessary concrete etc. However, when I appeared with my borrowed bucket and the stuff for the hole, he snatched it off me and went and made a much better job of it than I would have done.

I visited the hospital to see one of our 'Polio' boys, Chinamouthu who was an inpatient for the tenth time in his short life. I sat around most of the morning in a huge reception hall, waiting to be allowed in to his ward, and it was so different to English hospitals. The large cardboard cut-out of the Medical Director placed in the foyer for a start!

I watched the beautiful Indian women, walking through the hospital, wearing saris and with shining hair and generally looking like Miss World. Many of them carried rusted corrugated sheets, or ladders or buckets of sand, through the main foyer to the building site at the back, as they were the female labourers.

Chinamouthu was about 14 years old and had had ten operations for polio without any visible improvement, but this last admission to hospital was to decide whether or not further operations would be beneficial. Patients here have to have a relative or friend with them all the while to feed and care for them but there were very strict visiting times for other friends and relatives. Chinamouthu had found a nice fellow patient of his age, who was also handicapped as a result of polio. The boys told me with great pride that this friend's family were paying for his operation and hospital fee, and he was not a 'free' patient. A Canadian sponsor was paying for Chinamouthu's operations, but no hospital fee was charged, because he lived at the Orphanage. It didn't look very promising as far as his walking was concerned but it was hoped that he would be able to sit up straight at least. Chinamouthu's English was fairly good and he tried to explain to me about an upset he had had with his Surgeon. I was completely perplexed about it all, however, and without understanding what had really happened, I helped him write a letter of apology to this Consultant, which he seemed satisfied with. He still seemed to be optimistic about eventually being able to use callipers. I didn't speak to anyone in authority about him on that visit, and our time was completely taken up with the misunderstanding with the doctor. However, on a subsequent outpatient appointment I accompanied Chinamouthu and the doctor had sad news. He told me that we must tell Chinamouthu that he would always need a wheelchair to get about, because all the operations had proved unsuccessful. I thought that Chinamouthu would be devastated but possibly he had guessed the outcome, because he was incredibly calm and accepting of what I had to tell him. The doctor had suggested I find someone in England to donate an electric wheelchair, so that gave me something to think about.

We bought a baby back to the Orphanage when we left Chinamouthu, on the day of my first visit. This baby's mother's family had cast her out. The baby had been born by Caesarian section the week before, and was absolutely *minute*. I carried her home and I couldn't help comparing the homecoming with that of an English baby. There was no carrycot, buggy, disposable nappy, drinking cup, bath, nothing! She just had a rag nappy and a blue flannelette sheet round her.

Families for Children accepts unwed and destitute pregnant girls and provides full medical care before, during and after delivery of the babies. The girls like this little baby's mother would be encouraged to stay to care for her baby for the first weeks and after that she could leave with her baby or perhaps leave the baby with us to be legally adopted according to Indian law.

I'm ashamed to say that in spite of all these serious matters, I was at this time having occasional food 'fantasies'. One day I was photographing the seven little black hairy pigs that rooted about in the black mud by the side of the road (most roads actually) and I have to admit that I just couldn't stop thinking what a lot of bacon sandwiches they would make. However, I could still buy lovely cauliflowers - they are called cauliflowers in Tamil, too! With tinned cheese they made a good supper. The other delight of the week was a Varda, which is a sort of herby, spicy burger without the bun and sold in a café called Lechmi Villas. Apparently known as THE café in the village, the cooking was done by men of a very high caste called Brahmin, but I didn't think I could manage lunch in there. It looked distinctly unsavoury when I took the boys there on our walks, for a Pepsi and a bun. The food they produced looked and smelled very good, though, and I always bought one

59

or two of these Varda home for my supper. There were some very odd shops near the café but I usually headed to the town for the little shopping I needed.

The barber's visit to the Special Boys was particularly awful one week - he shaved them. *All* their lovely hair disappeared and they looked like a lot of aliens when I got home. I was so sorry for the way they looked. The ayahs insisted the boys didn't mind - they said they were just glad to get rid of the head lice, which was the reason they had been shaved. Anyway I was going to town so I bought them all a baseball cap to cover their heads, and they were *thrilled*. Of course it meant that everyone else wanted one too - the women teachers, the drivers, and even the elderly next-door-neighbour whose wife had thrown him out of their house. They all called at my house to ask for one.

My expedition to buy the hats was combined with a visit to Andrah Bank - a new Bank for me because I had had trouble with the original Indian Bank. As a result of my English bank being bombed in Manchester, my Visa card had been 'picked up' by the Indian Bank, and they wouldn't let me have any money here. However, at this new bank I asked them to cash a cheque and they just said, "How much do you want?". It was lovely, and reminded me of a time in France when the Bank Manager gave me money on the strength of my Kidney Donor Card.

A very dishy man here said, "How much do you want? Ten Thousand?". I laughed and said, "Yes, that would be nice" - thinking he meant pounds - and he meant rupees. Since this was one hundred and ninety pounds worth, I was just as pleased. He gave me this great wodge of notes and Raji and I walked calmly out of the Bank and collapsed in hysteria in the van. The money meant I could buy the water-purifying machine that I yearned for. (It ran tap water through what looked like an ultra violet light and it came out drinkable.) It cost one hundred and one pounds but I thought I could give it to the Orphanage Baby Room, when I went home, so it would be worth it. I know, you are

60

thinking I should have given it to the babies right away, but I cleared it with my conscience by thinking of the instructions the air hostesses give you, "Fit your own oxygen mask before you fix the children's'".

At the risk of being boring about How Hot It Was, here is another story: I was walking through town with no hat and wearing my glasses up on my head where I often lodge them. I stopped to look at the price of something and moved my glasses down and burnt my cheeks with the steel rims.

That was during a hot but successful shopping trip in Coimbatore. I bought purple and orange, woolly and hilarious Indian baby socks for my niece, Kate, in England who had written to say she was expecting a baby. Also a door curtain made of beads which I thought might discourage visits from the boys next door (but it didn't), and a mat for my bedroom floor. It was Election time again and so the town was fuller than ever with people and it took nearly two hours to get to town on the bus and even longer to get home. I found crossing the roads while in town a very real hazard and after several near-fatal incidences, I gradually adopted a rather cunning system, which was to stand me in good stead for the rest of my days in India. I simply looked out for a local, waiting to cross, and nipped in behind them and copied them in everything they did. I had to keep *very* close to them and be very sensitive to their sense of direction, which often meant adopting their style of walk as well, but it *worked*. I suspect that some of the women felt a bit menaced by my proximity but oh it was fun making the men edgy (Just a tiny revenge for their harassment of me?). It was difficult to get on a bus to come home with all my packages, and I was usually very relieved to get a seat at some time on the way home, or I think I might have collapsed.

Perhaps the Lord was also sending me riches via the mysterious Benefactor? A big Loaf of Brown Bread, arrived one day. What a joy it was. I loaded slices of it with fried tomatoes one day and scrambled eggs another and finally ate it up with cauliflower cheese. A highly coloured calendar and a huge watermelon accompanied the loaf. If this man *was* just keen on white women, you could say I was nearly a 'kept' woman. The tomatoes were misshapen and funny coloured, but tasted so good I wondered about growing some myself. The heavy rain falling daily meant instant bushes, leaves and shrubs where there had been none before. My 'bits and pieces' had taken root and multiplied outside the house and the pots that I bought for forty pence or so were wonderful fat terracotta beauties so the 'garden' *looked* a huge success, even when the plants were a strange assortment. The pots were made for storage of dry goods really and my visitors were very amused to see their new use.

I loved showing this 'garden' to an English visiting couple, called Patrick and Kate, who broke my weeks of no one English to talk to. They were ex-Volunteers who looked amazingly like my own son and daughter. The first time I saw their tall figures in the distance, walking towards me, I was quite shocked and got emotional. They coped with this strange and tearful woman welcoming them to Podanur and told me about their seven-week holiday which included this visit to Podenur to see if there were any of the same children and staff still here. How I enjoyed their visit. I made cauliflower cheese and fruit salad for their first supper with me, and they raved about it because they had had five weeks of spicy stuff and insisted the blandness was wonderful. I loved hearing about the work they did while they were here and also about their English lives - a self-employed physiotherapist and a designer, in London. They were impressed with the raised standards in the Orphanage and the condition of the children, since they had last visited.

They had come here via Ooty and while they were there Kate had been asked to do two days as a film extra - a nun - in a Peter Ustinov film called Stiff Upper Lip. She had been paid 1,000 rupees a day to sit about and 'look virginal and pristine' and they had focussed a lot on her beautiful clean nails. Patrick had enjoyed watching the filming and they urged me to apply for similar work, as they were short of white women apparently and the pay was wonderful.

Sunbeam and Indira, who was an FFC Board member and already a good friend to me, came to supper to meet up with Patrick and Kate again. Indira was the businessman's wife who was on the Board of Directors of the Orphanage. She was highly intelligent and talked knowledgeably and enthusiastically about all Indian matters - mystic and modern - and about women's role in India, and we all enjoyed each other's company very much. At supper time they teased me with "Shall we have red or white?" As we fell instead on chilled Pepsi. Indira had come bearing a bunch of hibiscus flower heads, which only lasted two hours but smelled and looked wonderful on the table, plus a beautiful big brown loaf, half a huge watermelon and some chapattis. She was excited to tell me of a group of young men who wanted to come to entertain our children, sometime soon. I was so pleased that evening to host a supper party and enjoy the company of such wonderful people.

CHAPTER TEN

The Church Youth Group Concert and some letters from the girls to their sponsors.

The Coimbatore-based Church Youth Group that Indira had told us about, arrived at Boys House the very next day, and said they would like to entertain us, then and there. I hastened to get the Special Boys into a van (16 of them) and transport them up the road to Boys' House, where the 'concert' was to be held. They were all so excited it was hilarious. We found most of their baseball caps (the ayahs had pinched some of them) and as the star of the Youth Group also wore one, they were well pleased with themselves. About a hundred boys and girls and staff sat in the sand for an hour and a half without a drink, a trek to the loo, or a quarrel and they just loved every minute of the 'concert' in spite of the downpour thundering on the roof. There was a chap with a mike and another with a sort of electrical console and the children were allowed to do a bit of a dance - (only some of them, mind). One or two sang with the mike, including Muthu who was blind and really fancied himself as a singing superstar. All in all it was a very successful evening and I *did* hope they would return - as they promised to do.

When I staggered in my door, following the concert, I found the floor awash with dirty water because the heavy rain we'd had, during the concert, had come through the tiled roof. A repairman called the next day and 'walked' up a coconut tree to peer over at my roof opposite, to see where

64

the leak was. He then descended and climbed up on to my roof with a couple of tiles and solved the problem. Well, I kept my fingers crossed anyway. By coincidence a second man called at the same time with a huge tank of something that was supposed to kill bugs, on his back. He *said* it was to kill bugs but the previous week, when he had sprayed everywhere, I unexpectedly slept all afternoon and the bugs went forth and multiplied. I think it was DDT in his tank. Haven't I have read nasty things about that?

Several of the girls wrote letters for the Families for Children Newsletter and I think you would like to read some of them? They were written in Tamil and then translated as closely as possible into English. Unfortunately the original flavour is a bit lost through the translation but nevertheless they constitute real feelings and partial secrets that the children had agreed to share with their sponsors.

The first was from Dhanabackum:

"I am very happy here and I like FFC very much. All the girls are like sisters and Jen and Sandra and Sunbeam are like mothers. I get everything I want from FFC. I would not like to leave this place. I am studying well and I am in the tenth standard. The others who are studying with me in the tenth standard are my best friends. And the best friends are Baby, Buvaneswary and Mala. We enjoy being together in our room and share secrets.

I am an average student of this home. The purpose I came to this home was my family's poverty. When I was small my parents handed me to FFC. When I was admitted here, Sunbeam asked me my name. I replied Dhana. All the other kids have nicknamed me Gunda Dhana (fat Dhana). When I was young I didn't have good food and I could only get 'canjee' (boiled rice with water). My family has only 'canjee' and they are happy with it. Compared to my family I am better here as I get good food, good clothing, a shelter and biscuits, Mixture (mixed deep fried salted items such as peanuts), sweets, fruits and so on. Whenever I am eating them I am thinking of my younger brother and sister. It sometimes makes me cry. My younger brother and sister wanted to study, but they couldn't continue after the fifth standard because of poverty. I have tried to admit my brother and sister in the home but there was no room for them. Sunbeam has replied that there was no place here. I was sad because they weren't admitted. Sunbeam went for a home visit and she saw my house. I thought she would take my brother and sister but she didn't.

After the home visit I made up my mind not to let me upset anymore. I am still wishing to have my brother and sister to be admitted here.

I am happy here but sometimes some girls would fight with me and they would not speak to me anymore. This makes me cry.

I want to be a nurse or an advocate. I want to be a nurse in order to help my mother whenever she is sick. My granny would like I become an advocate. A neighbour misused my grandmother's property. So she would like I take after the case. But I prefer to become a nurse and I study hard for this. My best wish would be to ride a bicycle. I am working hard in my studies but if you ask me what I learnt two days ago, I have all forgotten. My IQ is like that! What to do? I am not interested to go home. I prefer to stay here. Before I used to be bold and talked a lot but now I realise I have become very quiet. I have got a good reputation from my surrounding. I have written this with affection, as I would do it with friends. This is my story which is not complete."

Kavitha's letter:

"In our house we were five children. There was not enough money to feed all of us. My mother passed away when I was young. My father did not care about us. Only the sister of my mother was looking after us. This aunty was more interested in her own children.

I am feeling very happy here; most of all when I compare my present life to the one I used have at home. Even during the exams holidays I am not interested to go back home. I also get good food here. Specially I enjoy the different functions at FFC and I am good in dancing. Whatever I am asking at the office I get it. I would not like to leave this palace. My elder sister is already married. She is 23 years old and is living in Chennai (Madras). She is working as teacher. My elder brother is working at a booking office in Dubai. I am wanting to become teacher like my sister."

Manorajitham wrote this for us:

"I was in a critical position. I was doing some gardening work before coming to FFC. In my native place I was treated like a slave. My uncle sent me there. It was because I had no parents. At that time, I was brought to FFC by my uncle in a very sick condition. My brother is also here. Only after the death of my mother I was made to work. My father was psychiatric patient. After coming here I was better. Here I can forget all my bitter experiences.

I like to be here but I feel bad when the girls give me orders. I told the members of staff when the other made some mistakes. I agree with all the faults and I happen to know everyone so the girls teased me. I am an illiterate. My friends make comment about the fact I don't know how to read and I do all the things. I feel very bad and broken hearted. I like to study and I wish to talk in English more than the other girls. I wish that all the others to be affectionate with me. All the staff are good to me.

I enjoy to do the tailoring. When I arrived I didn't know anything but I am thankful to Sandra Mummy to have made me learning tailoring. I would like a machine and a room to stitch many bags and sent them to Sandra Mummy for sales and donate the money for the home. I wish this could be done. I don't want other to disturb me.

I want to have tuition at leisure time and study well. I wish I do as I wish. I want to thank for all the things having been done for me."

A letter from Poongodi:

"My family is very poor. It is the reason I came to FFC. If I had not come here, I might have died. My mother explained to me that it is on account of all the prayers she had performed that I could come here when I was eight months, on Christmas Day. As soon as I came, everybody was looking after me quite well. I am happy here and if my mother comes to fetch me I don't want to go with them. My friends are Jamuna Rani, Latha, Viramani, Gown. I like to play and spend my time with them. I am very fond of my 'Big Daddy' (my sponsor) and he is very fond of me.

One lady from FFC staff who has left now, has nicknamed me 'Bid'. I like Rachel, Jen Aunty, Melanie Aunty, Kate Aunty, very much. I am very stubborn and daring as I don't mind what others tell or think.

I don't like some girls as they always want to interfere, that is to criticise my family, especially my mother (she has no father) whom they called a 'road picker' (that is a woman from a very low caste whose living earning rest upon picking waste paper, plastic...) Because of their words I don't like them. I am now fourteen and I am studying in the ninth standard."

Malathy wrote this:

"This is a letter from your daughter Malathy. I am fine. How are you? I am orphan. I have no parents. Miss (the administrator) and all other staff working here are my mother and father and all my relatives. I don't like to stay in my house because my granny used to scold me. Whenever she saw me, she started to scold me. After my tenth standard I want to become nurse. It is my wish to become nurse. I am very happy at FFC and I don't need to worry wile I am here. All the other girls are really friendly with me and I am also friendly with them. I like the school where I am studying. Usually I don't get what I like but my friend Sangeetha brings me what I like. I am very fond of her.

More than five years ago I went to my grannies but I didn't like to stay there because other behaviour. As my granny has not come to visit me I think she must have expired. I have a lot of girl friends; but they don't help me when I am in trouble. Only Sangeetha and Shanti will help me. Whenever Sangeetha is scolding me, I don't bother because she always gives me good advices and she wishes me good. I sometimes think if she were my sister I will be very happy. Whenever I feel lonely I think of my dead father and mother and I start to cry. I think not having them any more is to be very unlucky.

When I was one and a half months old I was brought to FFC. Because of my mothers death I don't know what mother's love looks like. Whenever I watch other parents visiting their children at FFC I think I should be born just now. I sometimes thank that my mother will come and I look at the sky. Whenever I am crying I think that my mother might come and wipe tears away. It has been more than eight years that my parents passed away. After my parents' death no-one, no relative has come to visit me.

69

This year my school has arranged for a tour. I might go or I might not. If I tell more it will not be an ending story. As I am not willing to tell the whole story I prefer to stop here. I beg your pardon if there is any mistake.
Yours, loving Malathy".

Kate and Patrick knew these girls and were therefore delighted to meet up with them again and hear their continuing stories. They also told me of their excitement at seeing more of India this trip which whetted my appetite for doing the same. They said they would send me a list of where they had been - especially the best places - when they got home, and wouldn't leave it too long as my time left here was dwindling.

Time passed incredibly quickly here - even more so when I had company - and this in spite of the days seeming longer than at home. I suppose it was the early start to each day. Every day there seemed to be something startling to wake me up early. One morning, for example, there might be boys shouting 'Mummy' urgently in the glassless windows - they would want to remind me it was Drawing Competition Day or something similar. Another day it might be the cat being noisily sick. These typical starts to the day didn't exactly encourage me to return to bed and therefore I was usually ready to end the day in bed at about 9.30 p.m.

I was thrilled to be invited to a Silver Wedding celebration for Penny and Ceduric, the Anglo-Indian couple who lived down the road. They had hoards of Australian connections, some of whom had come to India especially to share in the celebrations. Cedric was wonderful to talk to. He explained so carefully to me why *he* didn't want to live in Australia in spite of all he heard from his 'rellies' about the'fridges, cars and material benefits. He knew he would hate the isolation of sitting in a house with only his immediate family living with him, and not the extended family that he loves, calling in as they do in India. He and

Penny are very lively, warm people and there were hundreds of friendly relatives and friends at their party.

Their four children were very much involved in hosting the party. They were all beautifully turned out - the boys in pale coloured suits and the girls in gold lame jump-suits and the like. The 'bride and groom' looked to me like children dressed up - they were so innocent and childlike somehow. I was shown the photographs of their wedding in the Sixties and it must have been the most sumptuous seen in the village at that time an eight tiered cake and everyone looking very glamorous and fashionable in a Western style. The beautiful Indian women looked particularly stunning in their mini-dresses.

There was a special Mass held in St. Joseph's Church (Roman Catholic) in Podanur, from 6.45 to 8.15 p.m. I was then offered a lift, crushed in the van with the Choir and their guitars, to the Silver Jubilee Hall where the bride and groom formally received us. The M.C. was the same man as was at their wedding and he did a speech about the wonderful loving relationship the couple still had. We toasted them in purple plastic egg cups full of the most (to me!) ghastly wine. I think there must have been 300 people and we all ate a lovely dinner of chicken biriani and sweet and sour sauce and noodles. Two huge watermelons were halved and held a mixture of chopped vegetables which was the starter-on-the-same-plate. For desert there were little cups of ice cream and chocolate sauce. I had been warned not to eat ice cream in India but risked it on this occasion without any dire consequences and with huge enjoyment!

A dear old gentleman kept bringing me things, including boiled water that he pinched from his son who had bought it for his own children. The rest of the adults drank tap water all evening. I was most grateful for the boiled water because it was by now 11 o'clock and still about 30 degrees. And I would have had about six enormous cups of tea, by this time, at 'home'. There was dancing in the style of English dances in the forties and fifties - The Gay Gordons, Valeta *etc.* and singing of songs like 'I've Got a Lovely Bunch of Coconuts'.

71

CHAPTER ELEVEN

More visits to the Exhibition, and yet another Amazing Haircut, prior to a weekend in Heaven

What an adventure my first visit to a *proper* hairdresser turned out to be. Vigi ('Laydies Beauty Parlour' it said) came recommended by Raji, our social worker, who had had her plait chopped off by her friend, the Vigi who owned the shop. She was a super girl, who welcomed me into her little salon and showed me a book of recipes and dresses that she made to sell as well as the normal hairdressing and beautician work. She sold me some anklet bracelets, which weren't quite like the ones I wanted for Holly and Jane, as they didn't have bells on them, but never mind - the sale helped her.

Vigi explained the circumstances of her little apprentice girl who was a thirteen-year-old from a very poor family, and who *had* to work. Her mother called in while I was there to inspect a pot which the girl had broken and which Vigi said must be paid for by the mother.

The salon was a sort of shed - the same size but not half as nice as my 'house' with a huge hairdresser's chair beside a sort of shrine with fragrant incense smoking away. When I suggested I was a bit too tall for her, sitting in this chair, and should I sit lower; she agreed but ignored the screwing device for that purpose and helped me to wiggle *myself* to be lower in the chair for her.

She then got the little apprentice girl to lay out the hair rollers on the earth floor - they were all the same size so I don't know why this was necessary. We then processed through to another shed outside. There I knelt on a chair and hung my head over a bucket while they threw small bowls of water over me, into the bucket, and then used the water again. Vigi was embarrassed that the water was cold but explained she had no heating system. Of course the water had been standing outside in the sun so it was hotter than at home anyway.

They had the most wonderful system for eyebrow plucking. It was called Chinese Threading and Vigi had a customer asking for it, from the college next door. Vigi abandoned me, wet hair and all, and started on this girl's eyebrows. She had the most beautiful face and eyes and sat down right next to me so I had a good view of this extraordinary method of hair removal. Vigi first made a sort of cat's cradle with some thread and plucked the brows perfectly by sort of rolling the thread across the straggly brows. Her client only squeaked a little and sweated a lot and it was all over in a minute or two. Apparently it is a centuries old system and you can Self-Thread with practice. Vigi laughed about the accidents you can have if you aren't skilled at doing your own eyebrows you speedily end up with none I would think.

Vigi proceeded to home-perm the hair on the top of my head and blunt cut the bottom and it don't come much blunter. I have had a 'curly perm' since about 1974 and really thought I would still have this style when I reached the Old Peoples' Home. However, the heat and the outbreaks of Nits, made me decide that Something Different Had to Be Done. Words cannot describe the result of her ministrations. I can only say that I looked just like an old British missionary or Julie Andrews *before* she left the Abbey. It was three days before I dared take my hat off - no, I jest. The consensus of opinion was that three-quarters of the village women reckoned their sister in law could have done much better.

Vigi collected up the huge bag-full of my old hair, which I had promised to at least three people who had put their hands in the praying position to ask for it.

In May I went on holiday. Jen, Marlene, Sunbeam, Raji and I, went to Mahabalipuram, near Madras, but still in Tamil Nadu, and had a wonderful weekend. On the day before we left, a little boy called Gregory gave me a very elderly birthday card with a big 7 on it. He gave me the sweetest smile and said it was for my birthday the next day. (The staff had noted my birthday from my passport when I registered.) Another kind person at the Orphanage offered to take me to vote in the Elections before I left. She said I could have my finger 'dyed' to prevent my attempting to have two turns, and she would get me the necessary voting slip. Just before I left for the station my still unseen, friend-of-all-Western women telephoned to ask if I would like any *blood* before I left on holiday. Then he rehashed his English and changed the offer to any *bread* if I needed it.

We set off at first light and travelled on the Tamale Nadu Express THE train in these parts, to Madras. There were stencilled roses on the walls of the train, and cushions and clean loos. The people on the train were 'townie' people that were very sophisticated and different to the people I met in our village, and there were many well behaved, huge eyed children everywhere. A wonderfully precise announcer told us where we were, on the intercom. She spoke in Hindi, English, Tamil, and Kerala, and all the information was interspersed with Tom Jones music. The scenery was 'biblical' and good food and fairly good coffee was provided for the whole of the journey. The cost of the seven and a half-hour journey was £9 and this included a mango drink, packets of biscuits and cake, cashews, a veggie burger/chutney/fried rice lunch, four cups of coffee and a cup of soup.

While the announcer was telling us that the "route bifurcates shortly" and other similar interesting facts, we were enjoying the beautiful saris and flowers worn by the passengers, the fast changing scenery and pleasant motion of the train. In Madras we took in our stride, quite calmly really, the fact that just as we were passing the Sheraton Hotel gates, our taxi hit a boy on a bike, reversed off him and hit a man in a new car behind us and then set off without comment from any of the parties involved.

We had a couple of hours' drive in the taxi and arrived in HEAVEN. The Ideal Beach Resort (Proprietor: P.M.Dharmalingham) was a series of 'cottages' by the most beautiful beach I've ever seen. The members of staff were soft-brown-eyed, lovely people and there was a tree-covered terrace with nets below the branches to keep the birds off the tables. There was the most wonderful food, which was very cheap, and huge bottles of beer for £1. (The best bit was drinking it unobserved by anyone who would disapprove of such decadence). The prawns were like baby lobsters and you could drink chilled coconut milk or have a seven-cup pot of super tea. (I think we had nine of these during our stay). My bill for saying "Have whatever you like - it is my birthday" - was £10. The staff even bought chunks of chocolate cake to the table with Happy Birthday written on it in dhal. There were real flowers all around it and I thought I was dreaming it all, because it was so beautiful.

That evening I sat alone in the sea for an hour and half and watched the sun going down, all red and purple, behind me, with the moon making a silvery path in front of me on the sea. I spent more time in the sea than anywhere during that break because the temperature was 40 degrees and the humidity incredible. I felt so deliciously CLEAN in the sea and all the Indian dust seemed to clear from me - it was a marvellous end to my 56th Birthday - I was *so* happy.

However, meanwhile, poor Marlene had succumbed to heat stroke and had to keep in the air-conditioned bedroom for the rest of her holiday. She said her 'quiescent' eczema had arisen and multiplied, too. However, it was definitely a case of being ill in comfort - laying in air-conditioning looking out on to coconut trees and beautiful beach.

Sunbeam enjoyed her first swim ever. She borrowed my Mothercare swimsuit (she is a slim sylph) and absolutely loved being in the sea. She was only happy to be there because no-one could see her, and I think this experience gave her the confidence to wear some Western clothes she had bought but never worn, on the return journey to Podanur.

Sunbeam and I visited frescoes and sculptures in Mahabalipuram that were from 640 AD and were wonderful. We also did some swift shopping in tourist shops, which were well stocked with the usual souvenirs. The tourists were nearly all Indians.

We saw a huge ball of stone, the size of a big house, which was perched on the hillside. How it stays there defies my imagination. Why doesn't it roll down? It was so large that people were sitting, resting in its shade but it looked so precarious I would have been nervous. Someone once explained the geological reasoning behind this phenomenon but unfortunately I was a bit tiddly at the time and the technicalities of it never registered.

I made enquiries about exactly what time the fishermen would set out to sea from a nearby beach and set my alarm for 5.30 a.m. The boats were wonderfully 'home-made' and a fascinating shape. However, the first disappointment was the fact that it was already light and they wouldn't need their own pretty lights on the boats. Then I met up with some mangy, nasty dogs. I walked bravely past, knowing they can scent your fear. I even kept walking (quicker and quicker) when I felt one nudging the backs of my legs but I was glad when I realised it was my wet skirt (wet from the sea, I think!), flapping against my legs.

There were no fishermen setting out in their boats but I could see a row of them crouched down at intervals along the edge of the waves, gazing meditatively out to sea, so I hurried on to see if there was going to be any action.

However, I suddenly realised that they were all 'answering the call of nature". I averted my gaze, shuffled past and came home, by the 'inland' route, burning my feet on the sand - ah well.

The return journey on the night train was very different to our earlier one. In Madras station, the perspiration actually ran off my elbows as I held my welcome cardboard cup of Nescafe in the hellish, yellow lit, dirty, crammed-with people, ghastly station. The amazing thing to me was that in spite of all this horror, there was still so much going on that was interesting and heart warming. Families were picnicking on the ground and sleeping in rows on and under the benches and all seemed to know what they were doing which, by then, I very definitely didn't. Sunbeam guided us into the train with enormous difficulty because of the hundreds of people trying to do the same, but we found our numbered beds eventually. The beds were three-foot wide 'shelves', and I was in the top one. I was sleeping so near to the 'dead' fan in the roof that I slotted my hat in it, out of the way, but unfortunately the fan came alive in the night and sliced the chiffon scarf 'strap' right off.

Whole families were crammed on these 'shelves' and the kids were so good. I didn't hear one squeak at all. They were drinking boiling hot coffee served from a bucket that went up and down the corridor which, back home, we wouldn't give to our children to even hold. They also cuddled each other and lifted each other up and down and were generally responsible for each other, all night. I was also impressed with how fastidious the travellers were; folding up their sheets   we each laid on our own   and carefully carrying toothbrushes with paste ready to use, to the loos. However, the loos this time were so bad that I couldn't use them as loos, let alone open my mouth to clean my teeth in there. I never did get to the bottom (?) of what Indian people carry a jug to the loo for. They assume a sort of religious air and stride purposefully towards the loo on trains with a jug in their hands. These jugs are provided in the restaurant toilets, too, but I must ask someone I know well, what the system is. I suppose a clue is that they never provide toilet paper.

Sunbeam and I had taken a quick look at the beach at Madras, before boarding the train and there was a lovely promenade, which had been donated by a European, years ago. While walking for a short time along this promenade, we saw Madras Cathedral, which was unfortunately clothed in scaffolding. The scaffolding was made of wood - it might even have been bamboo - so I photographed it for Bob - it looked like a cartoon!

One of the railway officials was a man from Podanur and Sunbeam talked self-consciously to him for a little while on the station. He hadn't recognised her in her Western skirt and blouse and they obviously made her feel a different person to the typically Indian girl she was in Podanur.

The porters at the stations were carrying huge loads on their heads, as do the women labourers here, but someone told me there are a fair amount of broken necks and back injuries because of this, and it is not surprising.

In spite of the pleasurable rest and excitement of being on holiday, it was nice to be 'home' and the boys were so pleased to see us back. It was easier to cope with the incredible heat, living in my little shed, too. I even felt able to resume the Walks with Mummy and on the very first one; we saw a huge tractor in a field. When I took the boys to look at it more closely, the drivers let the boys have a ride. Two lots of six boys hung on it at a time and they were ecstatic. They lined up to say thanks, without prompting from me. Heather - the American Volunteer - had joined us by then and while I was thanking the drivers, the tractor accidentally took off with her on board so that ended the proceedings on a high, I can tell you. They accelerated up a sloping field with Heather hanging on the side, looking like Boadicea. I shall always remember her waving regally to the boys as she disappeared up the ploughed field and into the distance.

I thoroughly enjoyed Jen and Marlene's visit, even though it was so much shorter than hoped. My six Tamil (Prayer Meeting) friends visited again when we were all just finishing a cauliflower cheese-to-welcome-you-to-India-meal. Well it was a fatal combination as far as getting the giggles was concerned. The Tamils couldn't believe their eyes or ears because I think they found us unusually 'merry'. They left after about a quarter of an hour's singing and praying, leaving us a present of seven mangoes and promising to come again soon. Marlene and Jen fell on illicit ciggies to help recover from repressing their hysteria.

Jen had found a cook for us, called Sue-Sheila. It seemed a bit of a waste of her natural talent for cooking Indian food, when they requested omelettes and chips for our first meal, but I thoroughly enjoyed them, needless to say. After the meal we unpacked my parcel from my Mum in Ipswich and I was pleased to distribute another present of balloons from my friend Esme. The Special Boys had the benefit this time and they couldn't believe how *big* English balloons were, and how much longer they last.

In the same parcel as the balloons, Shanthi, the teacher, was intrigued to see the newspaper pictures of the Queen on her birthday. She asked me, "What is her name, Mummy?" I couldn't get over people asking me about our Royal Family, and even *where* England was?

My mum had also sent me a new cafetiére that was wrapped in a newspaper giving up to date progress of Ipswich Town Football Team so that was a bonus, too. And who can believe I was delighted to find that she'd remembered the Scotchbrite cleaning pads?

Most of the boys went 'home' for the holiday in May, to any relatives they possessed, to keep them in touch. Scores of them had no family and had to stay behind and their annual treat was an outing to The Exhibition. This was hugely exciting for them and they promised I would love it, too. It had loads of commercial stands but apparently there were animals, snakes, astrologers and medicine men, and a fairground, as well.

When we arrived I was *nearly* as thrilled as they predicted, but it was pretty awful and it was only their enthusiasm and delight that made me so happy to take them. There was a fun fair, with side-shows and hundreds of stalls selling plastic goods, saris, shirts, and wonderful things to eat. Candy floss, ice cream, fizzy drinks, as usual, but also deep fried, spice filled delicacies and battered chillis and two-feet-across-poppadoms. I took seven boys at a time, week after week, to this Exhibition, until they had all been at least once. They forged their names on the lists I put in the foyer of the Boys House so I was never sure who had or hadn't been! It *was* wonderful, for me as well, every time I went. They were such dear little boys. I tried taking more of them on the bus at first but I couldn't tell if any of them had got *off* the bus, on the way, by mistake, as I couldn't keep them all in sight! There were seventy people at least on every bus and when we got off we had to walk about on a motorway to get from the bus stop to the Exhibition. As there didn't seem to be any rule about what side of the road they drove on, I had a lot of trouble keeping the boys safe, and together. The upshot of this horrendous experiment was the decision to take the sort of motorised bee, which held seven boys and me, and cost about £3 return - to and from the Orphanage door.

When we set out there were wall-to-wall smiles and excited chatter, and tears from the ones that couldn't come this time. One boy clutched a huge, battered polythene container full of water and another a bag of biscuits. They didn't know much English, of course, and, once when I asked, "Have you been to the Exhibition before?" someone said "Four o'clock, Mummy"!

They were so pleased to be going anywhere and just loved me so much for taking them out. The motorised bee had a shrine in the front with the old incense going and filling the air, and I think the prayers must work because we got there and back, many times, without mishap. You think motor bikes and oxen that are meeting you head on must hit you, but they don't, somehow. Coming home it was always dark. I would have one little boy nestled up with his head on my shoulder, two more with their hot little hands holding my wet with sweat hands, and another going to sleep so precariously next to the mad driver, that I feared he might fall out. Everyone who was awake had a huge smile, whenever I caught their eyes, and there was no doubt they had had the very best time.

At the funfair in the Exhibition, the rickety rides were sort of home-made buckets that spun round, and there was a huge wheel that thankfully they dared not go on. One darling boy, aged about 15, had Downs Syndrome and the typically sunny nature that goes with that condition. He insisted he *did* want to go on another awful bit of fairground apparatus in which you sat, without a seat belt, and went up and round in a circle, what seemed like miles above the ground. I pleaded with him to go on a nice little 'Noddy' car instead but he was adamant. When he climbed in and set off, we all hid our eyes at first and then watched in disbelief at his pleasure. He was *so* thrilled with it all and I shall see him, punching the air with joy, yards above us, and smiling his huge beaming smile, forever. The others went on everything *except* this dangerous thing, and ate everything they wanted, and I still had change from £6. The most memorable thing for me about this day out was that the boys were *children* in the loveliest way - avid to explore and enjoy all the different things on offer and so easily pleased with even 'grotty" things.

I had the pleasure of an outing of *my* choice one night. Heather asked me to meet her in Coimbatore to go to the pictures. I was unsure of getting there and back in the dark but managed it without problems after all. I even got a *seat* on the bus on the way there. Heather was waiting for me outside the cinema, and first of all introduced me to all sorts of snacks being sold opposite it. She knew all about the film

- called Waterworld - and filled me in with the details while we took stock of the audience who were *all* male and didn't take their eyes off us all evening. I was therefore a bit dismayed when Heather said she could only stay until the interval because she hadn't been able to tell her 'digs' people she would be late home - and they would worry about her. Anyway she headed for home and I was sufficiently intrigued with this weird film to endure the stares of the audience as I wandered about in the foyer alone in the interval.

I found one other woman who looked friendly enough for me to ask her about the absence of women in the cinema. She was with her husband and assured me that it *was* the custom for women to go to cinemas in India but a man almost always accompanied them and that was why Heather and I had been eyed up and down even more than usual. She showed me where the most delicious coffee was being served, and offered me a lift home. She said she owned a car with great pride - so few people had one. I think she went a bit pale when I said where I lived, and was obviously relieved when I didn't take her up on her offer to drive me home. I enjoyed the rest of the film and found the bus stop for return to Podanur without any trouble. I bought a bottle of fizzy drink at the bus stop and was drinking it when the bus suddenly arrived. When I jumped on it, though, several people shouted at me and I was embarrassed to find that the bottle should have been returned to the shop and I shouldn't have taken it away.

CHAPTER TWELVE

The Zoo, a Rat and a Cat, and visits to Delhi, Coonoor and Arnekati.

Muthu, a blind boy, had some difficulties in school at one time, and I didn't know what to think about him. He wouldn't eat his dinner and wouldn't do his homework. He said he was being picked on by the teacher and was generally fed up. He was about fourteen years old. Apparently when he was about eight years old a farm worker bought him in to the Orphanage. He had been herding goats for his living. He was now saying he would rather go back to that way of life, than live with us. He was intelligent and very musical and I hoped that a mouth organ I had just purchased for him in town, plus the visits of the Youth Group, which he loved, would help him over this disenchantment with life.

He and I talked a lot about his decision and eventually he agreed to remain with us, if he could go to the Zoo again. The Park was actually a pretty grotty Zoo - again not my best thing in the World, but we did see lions (three feet away), tigers, bears, eagles, herons, peacocks, fluffy-legged chickens, a paddy bird (like a heron), camels, snakes, parrots, Adjutant stork, and cockatiels. They were all viewed through fragile netting and were moth-eaten woebegone specimens. There were so few foreigners living there that at one time I was looking at this wonderful tiger (the only fit, young animal in the Zoo and I was near enough to see his eye-lashes!) and when I turned around, there were about twenty people looking at *me* rather than at the tiger. A woman nearby told me I was the first Western woman she had ever talked to. The cages were all very small and the public can get really close to all the animals. Muthu couldn't *see* anything at the Zoo, but he reckoned the smells and sounds, and tastes of the candyfloss and peanuts, made the Zoo his favourite place.

I had taken a dozen or so parties of boys to this old Zoo by now and routinely did a head count at intervals during the visits. One day, there had been 26 boys at the ticket office, 26 at the miniature railway, 26 at the ice-lolly stop, and 26 in the van for the return trip. All was well, and I relaxed on the drive home, knowing that a jolly time had been had by all. We drew up at the Boys' House, dropped them at the door, and to be honest I was pretty tired and for once just waved them goodbye, and didn't go in with them.

I saw Jamal greeting them and was disappointed to see him berating one boy and looking very grumpy but I learned after that he had quickly spotted that there were 27 boys coming in the door. Apparently a little boy from the town had watched us coming to the Zoo, over several weeks, and decided he'd like to live with us. He had stowed away in the van and told the boys to keep quiet about him being there. He then told Jamal that he had no mother or father and that 'Mummy' (me) had said he could live at the Orphanage. Jamal didn't think it was funny and gave him his bus fare home to town, immediately. Everyone else was in fits, including me, except that when I thought more about it, it is a bit sad isn't it?

Jamal seemed to think I was going to make a habit of this carelessness and asked me to put numbers on the boys' collars in future. I decided to ignore his advice and pretended I didn't understand him. Jamal and I had a good working relationship by then but had not got involved with each other's personal lives. However, I had become a very firm friend with Shanthi, the teacher of the Special Boys, whose classroom was adjoining my home, and she bought her little girl to visit me, and even invited me to supper at her home from time to time.

Shanthi said the doctor had told her to rest in bed for two months. She was pregnant but had to work as long as possible because her husband had lost his job. She explained that the doctor had told her she should drink extra milk and she couldn't afford it - until next month - she said. I gave her some money but feared that it might mean the floodgates opening, and sure enough her friend appeared shortly after this asking for financial help for a sick sister.

The two women that did the washing also asked me for money and even asked for the old saris that I had hung on my walls to make the room look pretty. They showed me the holes in their own saris and looked highly delighted when I took my ones down and gave them to them. Talk about humbling.

Every day there was someone like these women to 'talk' to, for a while in my apartment but I was very dependent on reading for entertainment and I eventually got a bit low on books. I found Dickens' 'Hard Times' in the Office, but decided the times weren't quite hard enough for me to tackle that. 'The Scarlet Pimpernel' and 'Goodbye Mr. Chips' were the last of the stock of paperbacks left in the Canadian Director's apartment that I hadn't read, and I even felt grateful to resort to them at the end of my stay. My survival kit of things from England, including the paperbacks, lasted pretty well on the whole. This included a wonderful bottle of moisturiser that my sister-in-law, Pat, had given me as a going-away present. After I had showered, I dived into my nightie and shot under the mosquito net over my bed. I sat under the fan and anointed my bites with Savlon and creamed the wrinkles with this lovely M&S moisturiser and was very sorry to use the last of it.

The *reading* in India was more of a *squinting,* what with only a 20-watt fluorescent light, but the supply of books was terribly important to me and without them I knew I would have definitely got on *my* nerves.

I continued to worry about Babu who had to be locked in most of the time for his own safety. He was often was so disturbed that he couldn't go to lessons. He didn't appear to recognise his friends and had to be fed and washed and exercised. After his new medication from the hospital he had been sitting happily in class for a whole day and giving me a most beautiful smile, now and then. He had spoken a whole sentence, clearly, one day. I was so pleased with this progress but when I took him some crisps a few days later, he ate the packet as well, and one morning I found him sitting eating my garden plants from Ooty before anyone else was awake.

Another boy that I worried about hated to wear his trousers and was always walking around our 'compound' with them slung around his neck. While I was talking to him about this one day, he diverted my attention by showing me a bird that had got caught in a bush. We ignored his half-clothed state and extricated it and it flew gratefully away, and only when the washing clothes girls told me it was the sort of bird that pecks your eyes out did I realise what a lucky escape *he* had had.

A Delhi visit was intended to be a business trip for Jen and Raji and a holiday trip for Marlene and me. However, Marlene continued to feel ill and wanted to fly home immediately, via Bombay, so the party kept reducing as we travelled north. Jen had decided she must accompany Marlene, and Raji would do the adoption business on her own. I would explore Delhi without them, which was a bit disappointing - particularly as I am sure if Marlene had taken my advice and drunk gallons of tea every day, she would have recovered. In spite of this disappointment, I had a most intriguing and interesting time, right from the day we left Podanur.

We all met at the airport and suddenly, without warning, the mystery donor of Food and Things appeared. He had been sending food and calendars and things all the time I had been there and I still hadn't met him - I had just sent thank you notes. He was a small, well-dressed man with a fair knowledge of English and admitted early on in our conversation that he was a Western Women admirer. Raji told me, sotto voce, that he had once called at the chemists and had *her* wedding photographs copied, but only the ones with English women on.

On this occasion he met us to give us a three-course lunch in several billy-cans. In the billy-cans were pancakes filled with dhal sauce, various spicy-flavoured rices and other delicacies, but since Jen didn't like the man, Marlene was feeling decidedly ill, and Raji had just eaten, I had to 'do the honours' with the whole of the Airport Reception lounge watching my technique of eating with no cutlery. The Benefactor didn't eat with me, either - it was highly embarrassing. The others didn't even feel like *talking* to this man, so I babbled on about vegetarianism, multiple sclerosis, dental floss and other unrelated subjects, and was never so relieved as when he shuffled out of that airport with his still nearly full billy-cans.

I had innocently bought some new torch batteries at the airport shop and these caused havoc all the way to Delhi. I even had to get off the plane at one point and wait on the tarmac to acknowledge them. I got third degree burns on my bare feet because I had 'got comfy' on the 'plane, before being summoned by the cabin staff who wanted me to admit to ownership for some reason. The tarmac at the bottom of the steps was scorching. I have no idea what damage these torch batteries might have caused if I hadn't owned up to them and the nice sea captain, who I eventually sat next to, didn't know either.

After Jen and Marlene's departure from Delhi to England, Raji and I went to the Marina hotel for one night but it was £24 each so I suggested we move to another, which was much cheaper and more interesting. Apparently Mahatma Ghandi's murderer had stayed at the second hotel which, it is claimed, was the oldest hotel in Delhi. It had been wonderfully updated and I immediately made good use of the lovely shower. A tray of tea in the room only cost £1. The buffet breakfast was free. I noted that the porridge, curry, and whole tomatoes were kept hot by kerosene lamps under their containers, and revelled in the luxury of linen table cloths and wonderful cutlery and four or five waiters lurking to assist us.

We met up with American Heather and her friend from the U.S. - they had been to Nepal and were full of how wonderful it was. Heather's friend was good fun and we shopped and had pots of tea together. I thought the shopping was the best I had ever experienced but Heather insisted that Kathmandu was even better. In the Delhi bazaars we saw dresses, nighties, silk pictures, elephants of all sizes, shapes and substances, silk saris, caftans, sequinned baseball caps, little cobras in walnut-shells, silver anklets, bindis (that you put on your forehead), shawls embroidered with silk flowers and butterflies, leather sandals engraved with gold, bangles and carved chess pieces and new and old books in English at a third of UK prices. Everything in the shops or on the stalls was dirty or sparkly, incredibly expensive or really cheap, and the heat and haggling over the prices made me buy and/or discard items in complete confusion.

I flapped about trying to fit my paper cut-outs of Holly and Williams' feet into various exotic shoes and slippers but the heat got to me in the end and I grabbed wooden elephants and wall hangings of elephants instead and staggered back to the hotel. The wooden elephants would be a problem to get home because they weighed a ton but some little ankle bracelets were a good idea. These are little silver chains with baubles hung on them which are sold for girls from baby size to adult. These bells are worn by a bride to make a little bell-ringing noise to get the husband excited when they hear her approaching the bridal suite.

In between the shopping trips, we saw the beautiful Lutyens centre with its sandstone Parliament Building, India Gate, and the Art Gallery. We saw both the Ghandis' tombs, and the BaHai temple, which was a fantastic white, lotus-shaped design similar to the Sydney Opera House. We finished the day with a lovely supper in Nerula's - an American-styled restaurant - that sold Indian beer called Kingfisher, whose label boasted It's Thrilling when Chilled! And so it was. I was totally thrilled by bedtime.

I still felt worried about the cost of the second night's accommodation, even though it was cheaper than the first night, and had talked Raji into moving again. This time we went to a dingy place recommended by someone at the Orphanage. It was so late in the day when we found it, that we had to agree to a room with one double bed and Raji and I slept together - a first time for me, but Raji appeared quite used to it. If she was fed up with me for being so penny-pinching, she didn't say, and we were certainly awake long enough for her to complain. Apart from the overwhelming heat, the fan hiccupped through the night in a most disconcerting way, and in spite of being so tired; we slept poorly in the unsavoury surroundings.

The next morning I was taking a trip to Agra to see the Taj Mahal - Raji was due to go to a meeting about an Indian/Canadian adoption. It had been such a terribly hot, uncomfortable night and then I awoke at 5 a.m. to hear her say, "Jenny, I have loose motions and there is no water in the taps..."

Later I had a minor triumph - for me - because I managed to get the water to come out of the tap by turning it anti-clockwise. I don't usually have much joy with those sorts of technical plumbing problems.

Things got better for me during the day but Raji, poor girl, had to grapple with a lecherous Passport Officer in Madras to get the adoption papers finalised. I was fascinated to hear that she had gone to the receptionist in our 'hotel', before 6 in the morning and asked him for medication for her diarrhoea troubles. He not only supplied the pills, but he also fell in love with her and sent her letters for months afterwards much to her husband's annoyance and her amusement.

The next day Raji went off into the heat of the day to do business for Families for Children in the government office that processes adoptions. A small number of children are placed with adoptive families who are either orphaned or abandoned and the adoptions are al approved by the Indian courts. Where possible our children are adopted within India, with handicapped babies usually being adopted in Canada or the USA. No charge is made to the adoptive couples - FFC pays the cost.

Meanwhile after seeing Raji off to her meeting, I met Heather and we set off for the Taj on a tourist bus. We left the hotel at about 6 a.m. and there were men in the street shaving themselves, and each other, and 'urine-going' as the boys in Boys' House describe it. The parts of the city that we drove through were depressingly dirty and decrepit and the countryside wasn't nice, either. All the puddles, rice fields and rivers were purple or bright green-coloured, and you couldn't breathe in some parts of the town or country because of the pollution; kerosene, loos, exhaust etc. The signs. all handmade, even the huge billboards - were hilarious: Jain's Happy Nursery School, English Apothecary, and Poopalley Medical Supplies for example.

The bus driver asked us to write our ages and signatures in an Accident Book on the bus just in case. It was a slightly more comfortable bus than the local buses in Podenur, and I enjoyed the luxury of an assured seat, but the driver was either lucky or more skilful than the near misses suggested.

We visited tombs on the way there, and one was memorable for a tablet engraved with the wish that God would 'Purify the Heart and the Genitals', and 'If You Bring Babies into the Temple, Will you make sure they Behave'.

Heather wouldn't come into the temples because of her religious beliefs but I was intrigued and since there are not many Hindu temples that Christians are allowed to visit, I didn't miss out on any of those that *did* allow us in. The

Head Teacher at our village school in Podanur told me that in his opinion Indian people are ignorant in the main and they need symbols to get in touch with any God. He reckoned that their silent prayers and rituals with offerings of rice, incense and flowers were appropriate to their simple minds. Their temples are certainly very colourful and the smell and dramatic symbols make them memorable. Incense is used almost exclusively for worship in India and the fragrances serve a serious spiritual purpose in creating the right mood for their prayers. Ash denotes the impermanence of life and is often doused on a person; women and girls (not widows) traditionally wear flowers in their hair every day and both men and women have a "kum kum" or "bindi" - coloured spot - between their eyes. Visitors to homes are often given a bindi, when they leave, to wish the person happiness in their married life. Another Indian friend told me that she felt Hinduism is a personal interpretation of reverence to God - any God.

The 'comfort stop' at a tea-room, was memorable for the fact that the milk had to be strained as well as the tea because of the flies and leaves in it, and there were mangy monkeys everywhere! Our bus driver was pleased to meet Heather to talk about America because his cousin lived there. He asked if she knew the 'Hill Station called Colorado?'

We had lunch on a terrace, which was at the end of a flight of stairs and situated among some treetops. We ate with our hands, of course. Lunch here was mango chutney, rice and dhal curds. This was delicious but what looked like a dormouse on wings cruised about while we ate it, which was a bit nerve-wracking. I met a chap called Keith from Felixstowe - which is 11 miles from my hometown - but he wasn't as excited as me about this experience and he didn't really want to talk to me because *he* had loose motions too. He wasn't even amused by some very unusual sari-clad women walking about, so I composed a poem about them to compensate for his reluctance to chat.

There were girls from Mahari
In a strange sort of sari
It's a shock from the back -
It's tucked in their crack!

A lady in one of these saris was selling Indian, sparkly saris. I didn't actually notice the back of her own sari because I was intrigued with the trainers she was wearing with it! She said she had unfortunately sold out of the Wales I wanted   Muslim Veils. I have to say my Indian pronunciation was most probably just as likely to lead to misinterpretations.

The Taj took my breath away - literally. I was tearful immediately I saw it because it is so beautiful in a pure and pearly way and you can feel the love and emotion that inspired it. I find famous buildings are sometimes a disappointment when you see them for real but the Taj Mahal is even *more* beautiful than you think it will be. I could quite see why Lady Di sat moping on that seat when she saw it - it must be the most staggeringly beautiful landmark in the world. It is actually a huge white marble mausoleum, adorned with calligraphy, studded with turquoise, jade, and coral, and surrounded by gardens laid out in what someone told me was Persian Charbagh style. You left your shoes in a shelter, for five rupees, and joined hundreds of people walking slowly through one of the three entrances, south, east or west. You could go in from dawn to dusk and it must have been heart-achingly beautiful at either of those times. When I first saw it, in the middle of the day, I was filled with a sort of joyfulness. It has a sort of sensuous beauty. The sad love story behind the building of the Taj was in our guidebook but was confirmed by a university student who 'adopted' me in the, by now, expected way of Indian people. She told me that long ago - in 1632 - the Mogul Emperor Shah Jahan learned of the death of his beloved wife, Mumtaz Mahal and was devastated. He had been married for eighteen years and she was his favourite wife who never left his side in all this time. She had died giving birth to their fourteenth child. He had been a very valued emperor and was famous not least for his passion for delicately wrought architecture. He therefore decided that his beloved should be buried in a tomb of timeless beauty. A poet of the day said that the Taj Mahal was designed as a, "tear that would hang on the face of eternity". Twenty thousand craftsmen worked on the Taj and precious, and semi-precious, stones were brought from all over the world. The white marble shimmers against the blue sky or glistens under the moonlight and is inlaid with jade, lapis, amethyst, diamonds and mother of pearl. For over thirty years architects and master craftsmen worked until it was completed in 1653 and by this time the deceased wife had become known as Mumtaz Mahal, or Light of the Palace, and Shah Jahan had been overthrown and imprisoned by one of his sons in Agra Fort. He lived out his days looking over the river to the Taj Mahal and when he died, in 1666, he was he interred beside his beloved wife. Because she had died in childbirth, she is considered a martyr, and prayers are said at the tomb, in the cenotaph chamber.

Our bus tour only allowed us a couple of hours there and I was so disappointed when we drove straight to a horrible old garage nearby to have the windscreen of the bus repaired. We all sat in the bus for a sweaty hour while they fixed it and I would so have loved to spend this valuable hour, ten minutes away, at the Taj Mahal, instead of sitting in intense heat with a lady with a moustache who was probably the only Indian I met with no wish to know "what is your native country?" and ignored me.

While Heather visited friends, I went to India Gate to try to find my Uncle Robert McCombe's name on the memorial built by the British. It is covered with the names of regiments (including Kent Cyclists) and many of the names of the men who served, but I could only find Royal Horse and Royal Field Artillery, which was his Battalion.

Did you know that 70,000 Indian soldiers died in World War 1 and 135,516 British? The names of those killed on the northwest Frontier and in the Afghan War in 1919 are engraved on the arch and foundations of India Gate.

I went back again on the second day to search for Robert's name, and got 'adopted' by a pleasant young man, called Annirudddha Chatterjee who wanted me to stay with him and his parents next time I was in India. He also wanted me to persuade his mother that he *could* marry an English girl who he loved and who worked in a local leprosy hospice. She was from Durham. However, he strongly disapproved of a picture of my daughter and her husband because he thought Steve was an Indian. I think he was a bit confused about mixed-race marriages. We discussed the whole issue walking along broad pleasant pavements between modern banks and offices, and my new friend commented on the English walking speed, which he found amusing having noticed it before in visitors to India. He made a map for me of how to get to the airport and I dutifully repeated the instructions I should give the taxi driver and I was sort of relieved to say goodbye to him, he was so doubtful that I would manage by myself.

It was probably because of my solitary state that I was similarly 'adopted' by Australian Renee Sorenson. She spotted me in the airport and interrogated me as to my immediate plans, my history and future plans in a friendly, if 'bossy' way. As soon as she knew I wanted to stop over for one night in Bangalore she insisted I share a room with her and go to meet Sai Baba. Renee was amazed that I had not heard of this World famous, religious leader. She was a devoted follower and was visiting India for the third time just to see him. His Headquarters were at Whitegates, just outside Bangalore. We stayed in Bangalore in a mock Tudor hotel with a very Colonial feel about it, and Renee was a very amusing companion. Early the next morning we set out in a taxi, calling for an American friend of hers at another hotel nearby. This rich American boy was very disillusioned and fed up with India and wanted to go home! He was a devotee of Sai Baba but everything about India appalled him and he was even more distressed the morning I met him, because his expensive boots had been stolen while he slept in the hotel. However, Renee pacified him and repeatedly promised that the sight of Sai Baba would compensate for everything that had happened. Sai Baba apparently tours the World, establishing colleges and hospitals and promoting his gospel. When he returns to Whitegates, disciples who call him The Second Jesus meet him for prayer and praising and he gives some audiences to individuals. Near to his palatial home he has built a large college for boys and a hospital that takes patients who are believers.

On our arrival at the gates of the Reception area, I was amazed to see hundreds of Westerners in rows, kneeling or sitting cross-legged. There were men and women of all ages and a few children, and all were silent and most had their eyes closed. Some chanted softly but most appeared to be praying quietly. Many of the women wore beads and saris and were aged about fifty years or so - definitely in the menopausal, 'finding themselves' category. We joined a row of people, and sat cross-legged for ages, waiting and getting up to put some blood back in our legs, from time time. Before we joined the waiting disciples, we had what I would call 'health food' in a very clean refectory where we met people from Holland, Denmark, and America. Some were in parties of a dozen or so and wore matching neckerchiefs or badges. I didn't meet any English but understood from the Dutch woman I sat next to at the meal that there were a large number of devotees in England, including famous actors and actresses. Everyone I talked to seemed articulate and well educated and many were full of fun, too.

The air of excitement and tension grew as time passed. I couldn't believe how comfortable everyone else seemed to be and obviously not having the troubles I experienced - numb posterior, cramp, dead legs, etc. I had been promised all sorts of more pleasurable physical thrills, the minute I set eyes on Sai Baba, though. Suddenly there was an audible in-drawn breath from hundreds of people, and a man looking incredibly like Michael Jackson in an orange nightie walked slowly down the row about three away from ours. He had a big halo of black, curly hair and was brown-skinned and about 70 years old, in a 'hard to tell' way. He had black, shiny darting eyes and I concentrated like mad on being impressed by him, but nothing happened. Around me, though, women were crying, noisily or silently, and smiling and waving at him, or throwing flowers in his path. Some people were raising their children, many handicapped, for him to touch them. He smiled benevolently and walked slowly up and down a few rows and then got into a huge car and was borne away. Renee was ecstatic that she had been so close to him this time, and was perfectly satisfied with her visit. She had had several personal interviews with him, over the years, and interesting correspondence. It seems she can think of him, when she is in Australia - even just walking around the supermarket - and can experience spasms of pleasure and warmth and blush-inducing euphoria for several minutes. She took me to a friend of hers, who lives for six months of the year in a rented cottage, near Whitegates, just so that she can see Sai Baba. They gave me a reading list and seemed to forgive me for not becoming an instant convert, but urged me to research and learn more about him when I returned to England. The thoughts that they gave me to take away with me were: Hands that serve, are holier than lips that pray/ The life of a person that does not love his mother is a wasteful life/Cows are a symbol of Mother Earth, Mother Love - motherhood generally. They also reckoned that *chanting* is an essential part of prayer and praise.

These new friends made me carrot juice and a meal called Sweet Pongal: they boiled rice and added brown sugar, ghee, ground and chopped cashews and dried grapes. While cooking and eating this, they planned their next attempt to see Sai Baba.

I returned to central Bangalore to have a look around. Unhappily, and for the first time, I felt I couldn't cope with being touched, or leaned against, or stared at, by the many Indian men who think white women should endure this treatment. I had by this time adopted a 'funny walk' which usually protected me, but in Bangalore for some reason it didn't seem to work. All you do is swing your arms back and forth, but in an outward arc, as you stride along and see them coming towards you. This is usually sufficient to make the men have to walk wider of you than usual and contact with your body more difficult for them. I just stayed long enough to appreciate that Bangalore was full of colonial architecture with wonderful trees and bushes that were well established but I finally fled to my mock Tudor bedroom and read under a desultory fan. My book at the time was Far from the Madding Crowd. I was enjoying it so much I thought I would read all evening, too, but the light bulbs weren't bright enough in my room or in the hotel restaurant, so I went to sleep very early instead.

On my return to Podanur lovely Heather arrived at my house with two huge bags of goodies that she didn't need as she was returning to Minnesota after nine months in India. She was escorting one of 'our' little boys for adoption by a Detroit couple. There was a chance she could 'pick up' another little boy in Madras. An American family was adopting him and it would save thousands of dollars in escort fees if she could escort him, but she hadn't had confirmation of the arrangements, from Canada, so far. I was so impressed with her confidence in her own ability to look after *two* little boys all that way.

She offered me bags full of odds and ends like sweeteners for tea, a huge, black T-shirt, an eight inch high Christmas tree with decorations, a length of awful material, six American paperbacks, and a real silk, green and beautiful sari which someone had given her. (I thought I might have this made into a blouse or something because I certainly could not bear the heat when wearing a sari.) The second bag had eight Billy Graham-type books of a definite ecclesiastical nature but I thought I would see how desperate for reading material I got.

I knew I would miss her visits but the next excitement in my life was the erection of Harry's House and on the morning of her departure, with no ceremony at all, the building of Harry's House commenced.

Harry had sent money to build a dormitory block for the little boys - so that they didn't have to grow up among the older boys. All the four to seven year olds would live in this new house designed especially for them, in 'my' courtyard. I was amused - and impressed of course - to see a small woman arrive and sit down in the middle of the yard, breast feed her baby, lay him in a sacking hammock between two trees, and start to dig the footings of Harry's House. Several men followed her but when they arrived she stopped and made their breakfast before joining in with the labouring again. She worked in a sari, of course, and had the usual heavy plait of beautiful black hair down her back. At first she was a bit hostile to me but she relaxed after a bit and accepted some odds and ends I offered her - albeit with the usual bored nonchalance that Indians have when you give them anything. It turned out she was a friend of Parvati who is a noisy, smiley woman who works in the Girls' House.

On a walk around the village with the boys one day, Parvati - an ayah at the orphanage - invited me in for tea. I didn't know her very well but no one had ever asked me in for tea, off the street so to speak, so I was thrilled at the invitation. At first I gestured at the twenty or so boys I had with me and declined gracefully, because of them. However, Parvati said they were welcome too! So we all packed into her tiny room with its earth floor and no furniture to speak of but a television in the corner. The boys all sat down, *very* close together, and watched the television while Parvati and

I drank tea and talked. To my amazement, there on the television was a framed photo of an Ipswich friend Linda, a social worker from my hometown. She had come over with Jen two or three years previously, for a working holiday, and Parvati and she had become such firm friends that she had this picture in pride of place in her room. Linda and I had had long chats about dealing with 'nits' - in India and in English schools - and it wasn't long before that became an important issue in my life again.

The Director of the Orphanage faxed from Canada to say she didn't agree with my method of dealing with head lice in Boys House. I had put up posters in the washrooms with a giant nit with a cross over it and another picture promoting a bottle of special shampoo and a third picture of a shaved head with a cross over it. I thought this had been working ever so well, since the ayahs had taken notice of the illustrations, the nits had gone and the boys' wonderful hair had been allowed to grow back. However, the Director felt that the shampoo was dangerous and, anyway, she said, the boys *liked* their heads shaved in the hot weather. I gave in to her superior knowledge of the country and the people, but stood my ground over the ice-cubes, which the staff here didn't agree with either. I had been producing orange-flavoured ice cubes in the very hot weather and the boys were delighted with them but the ayahs declared them dangerous. I kept up production in spite of their fears, and hoped desperately not to be found guilty of damaging their health.

There was one ayah with whom I didn't see eye to eye from time to time - on small things like the ice-cubes but also our big difference of opinion was over The Stick. She always sat with a wopping big stick by her side and I had argued with her about the need for it on several occasions and once felt sufficiently worried about it, to break it up and throw it on the kindling pile. She took my dramatic action with a gritted-teeth-smile, but I felt she would probably get another before long and one of the other ayas told me she had. Her argument was that she never actually *used* it - it was symbolic - and my lack of Tamil language prevented me doing anything more than *symbolically* taking The Stick away each time. One night, as a result of a rumour relayed to me by another ayah, I got up at about 11 p.m. and walked in the dark to the Boys House to find a Dickensian scene in their bedroom. Two senior boys and this ayah were yelling and hitting boys with sticks. There was crying and screaming from the boys and I couldn't believe what I was witnessing. The senior boys tried to hide their sticks and the ayah stared at me belligerently when they saw my horror and amazement at what was going on. This was the only time I actually *saw* bullying of this kind, and it gave weight to my insistence that sticks were never to be used, symbolically or otherwise.

I had a visit from a rat one night. I had just enjoyed another dinner cooked for me by Sue-Sheila and had washed up and sat down to read when the electricity failed again and the lights went off. I found a torch (enormous red plastic one, which was a Special Offer in a Sunday paper before I left home), and ignored the fact that without the fan, I would sweat and sweat while I read, and then He arrived. He stood in the doorway, paused (pawsed?); and then walked in so casually, you'd have thought he'd been invited. I felt as if he might take his coat and hat off, he looked so much at home. I called out to him - "OK" then screamed - and he shot out again fairly quickly.

The next day I told the staff and they immediately surrounded my house with 'Rat Medicine'. I don't think anything furry could have got near the house for years. On reflection, next day, I thought I had better get it removed, in case the handicapped boys found it and ate it! Oh dear! I tried to explain my dilemma to the cleaning lady and asked her to sweep it up out of their way. She reluctantly did as I asked but she didn't know whether I really meant her to do it and certainly didn't understand why. She and I had a lot of laughs about language. She was a hoot, she thought that if she shouted loudly enough at me, in Tamil, I would understand her. I too, shouted - but in English - however we never understood a word of each other.

To go back to Sue-Sheila: she arrived at about 6.30 and went home at 7.30 p.m., leaving the kitchen sparkly and clean and two or three dishes of something delicious waiting on the table for my supper. First of all, though, she made me a cup of tea. I can't tell you what luxury it was to have one *made* for me. I was usually typing away when she arrived and she would glide in and say, "Where have you put your tea powder, mum?" or, "Would you like chapattis today?" I got into trouble for getting up to answer her enquiries when she called out to me from the kitchen. She would say, "Be sitting nicely, mum!"

She said she would come in four times a week for two pounds. It wasn't the food I liked so much as her company in the evenings. I read, or typed or listened to the radio while she worked, but it was lovely just hearing someone pottering about in the house, after dark. The Orphanage staff insisted on calling her my servant - as if I didn't feel guilty enough having these little banquets of omelettes and curries prepared just for me. She came, rain or shine, and sometimes brought her nice teenaged daughters with her. These girls were the cause of anxiety and sleepless nights because, as a single parent she would be responsible for dowries for her girls. She explained what poor prospects they had because they had no money for the saris and gifts necessary to make a good marriage arrangement.

The rains commenced and whew - didn't it rain? But it soaked away quickly and left a nicer temperature than before. It was still hot enough to make sweat drops drip off my extremities. The mould, which followed a few days of the wet weather, attacked even my sun hat and I had to keep scrubbing it clean. Another of the mould casualties was the chaise longue in the sitting room. It was a rather lovely old wooden piece of furniture, un-cushioned, and I was relieved when a scrub and exposure when the sun was high, cleaned it up.

I made a successful telephone call to England during a hot afternoon. It was marvellous how easy it was on one day - but how impossible the next. When I say *easy* I must tell you that I had to reach through a grill in the wall to extract the telephone and dial the number, in the full glare of the sun, with at least six very retarded girls, behind me, nipping and pulling at me and lifting up my skirt in full view of the people in the street. Since I had long given up wearing undies, this was a particularly dangerous trick.

The children in Special Girls were all particularly excited and happy that day because the Canadian Director, Sandra Simpson, had sent them a Music Centre and their rather Spartan, though new, quarters were resounding with all sorts of music at maximum volume. At the same time as this gift arrived, Sandra's daughters sent another donation of 150 school bags and I was asked to paint each with their Orphanage number in luminous green paint and with a too-big brush. Their initials and their standard in school needed to be marked in Roman numerals on every bag. The paint had to be thinned with kerosene and I felt distinctly queasy by the end of the day. They were a particular delight to our children because the other pupils that didn't live in the Orphanage already had them.

I can't spell or pronounce the name of the village where we went, near Coonoor, but there were fifteen boys and three adults in a VW-style camper van and it was Very Hot. There had been no electricity in the night so Mummy wasn't at her brightest at 7 a.m., having lain in a pool of sweat most of the night, awake. But the excitement was infectious and the boys were all wearing their best clothes and baseball caps and their SMILES. They were particularly delighted when I wore a sequinned baseball cap that I had bought in Delhi.

One or two were too naughty to be taken out (staff opinion, not mine) and the consolation balloons I offered

102

did not stop their tears at being left behind. I don't really know where they could have sat, on reflection. We were packed to the ceiling. Two had to sit on the floor where they couldn't see a thing, two had had polio and their legs were useless and little, so balancing on the seats was a problem. Several went straight to sleep with the motion of the van so they kept falling off the seats, too. The driver made no allowance for all these things and we screeched to a halt, turned corners at speed, but in spite of all this it was the best Outing I have ever been on and the boys thought so too.

We went 50 kms. to a dam near Coonoor, where there were flower gardens and a mini zoo and an aquarium and a wonderful viewpoint where we picnicked. Our Ayah produced a delicious meal from big steel drums and we ate the food on big leaves, with our hands, and held the water can for each other to wash, *after* the meal. We had five minutes worth of motor boat (in two sessions) on the lake - with life jackets I was relieved to see - and we came home by four thirty.

I'm not sure why it was so short a day because I heard there were illuminations later and we didn't 'do' the miniature railway or snake park, but suddenly we were being packed in the van, by the driver, and heading for home. The boys were all still smiling away. If they aren't smiling they are gazing adoringly at me - I was getting used to it but it still made me self conscious.

When I looked in on the boys at about 8.30p.m. They had all gone to 'bed' - lying on the floor asleep - and one had a little lizard draped fetchingly on his forehead. My English was beyond the driver's comprehension so I tried to find out from someone else why we came home so early but it remained a mystery. The driver was a lovely man who kept asking me to, "Look at your *telephone* and tell me the time" so perhaps he wanted to get home early for a date.

Most of the boys on the outing were retarded but they still managed to guide me (on purpose) into the Gents, instead of the Ladies, they pointed out that the back of my trousers had come un-stitched, and asked me on the way home as to whether, if they caught my nits, they would be white ones? And similarly, if I caught their nits, would they be black ones?

Indians don't think it is rude to stare and I got used to them stopping, right next to me, and staring into my face. Anyway there was one boy (not one of 'ours'), while we were on the Outing, that really got on my nerves, doing this staring. I finally came the English MemSahib bit and haughtily told him to clear orf, attempting to be very posh and authoritative, but he didn't respond. He then told me that I had something 'foreign' on my nose. (He said it in Indian, but you know how you immediately feel there must be something gruesome - like spinach or a bogey - on you?) Well, it was a lump of candyfloss that had got there when one of my little boys had tried to give me some of his. This will explain to you how closely the general public examine foreigners.

On the Monday afternoon following that Outing, one of the boys brought me a present from them all, for taking them on the picnic. It was a very poisonous-pink, plastic doll with a luminous pink foam dress covered in sequins. I rather think Marimuthu made it for me. He was 24 and could not walk at all, and he couldn't lift his arms high enough to even brush his hair, either. (I shuddered to think of his problems when he had nits).

When I went to town one morning I had to wait ages for the bus. I had been told three different times of take off for this bus, so I was quite resigned to wait at the bus stop, until one came along. A man who looked like my Uncle Fred - Indian style - examined me in detail, as people do in this little village. He had silver hair and whiskers and a sort of military air about him, and he stared and stared at me. Well, he then went on to carefully examine the bananas on the nearby stall, bought some and gave them to me without a word or a smile.

The shopping expedition that day was pretty successful. I bought a kitchen clock for £3, locks and keys and things for Boys' House, and a watermelon. The bus stop experience at the town end was not so pleasant, however. A man was demonstrating his prowess with a huge snakeskin whip. He was asking for money after cutting his arm with the whip in about ten weals from the wrist up. He made straight for me when he had finished, to show me and beg for money, but I had anticipated it and was purposefully looking the other way by then and hastening away.

Boys House was 'fulltight' as they said in the Orphanage, in May. We were back to 100 and 48 more were due to arrive soon. I took in a new arrival to Boys House one morning. A policeman had delivered him to the Office and he came with me to Boys House, crying all the way - out of huge, grief-stricken eyes. He was frightened to death of me, I think - he probably hadn't seen a white grandma before. He had a mentally ill mother, his father had 'expired' as they said in India, and his small brother had also 'expired' recently because of malnutrition. By teatime, however, he was laughing and relaxed. Mary (chief ayah) said she would keep him off school and feed him up for two weeks. I thought this was wonderful. I had been mentally devising a 'buddy' system for newcomers like him, during my sleepless nights, but when I put the suggestion to Mary, she just said, "Oh, they Pick Up, Mummy". I soon saw what she meant.

The adorable little Sachin was seen off from India to Detroit. I accompanied him and American Heather to the local airport. The adoptive parents were meeting them at Detroit airport. Sachin slept all the way to our airport in the van (an impossibility I would have thought). His eyelashes were fanned out on his chubby, flushed olive cheeks, and he clutched a plastic grand piano, that unexpectedly played Greensleeves with the motion of the van. He was wearing

105

trainers, which you didn't often see in India, so I thought someone must have kitted him out appropriately from America. It was so lovely to look at him and know what a fantastic life he would have in America, compared to life on the streets here.

At the airport I wore the sari that Heather had bequeathed to me, to make her laugh, and I hope she appreciated my gesture, because it had taken three women to wind me into it and I nearly exploded in the heat, wearing it. I was sad to see her go.

Nilgri Hills Visit

I went on a lovely home visit with Sunbeam, to possibly collect a new boy for the Orphanage. We went to a tribal village in the Nilgiri Hills to visit a woman who had previously come to the Orphanage to ask us to take in her last son. She had had five other boys and her husband had deserted them ages ago. None of the boys had been educated and it was her wish that this one should learn to read and write, even if it meant she had to live without him, which was going to be a great sacrifice on her part.

We went about 30 kms in the van and it seemed much further because the roads were terrible. However, we travelled through absolutely beautiful countryside - very different to the area in which we lived. The driver told us that elephants, tigers, monkeys and many other animals lived here. The flowering trees and bushes along the way were strange to me and exotic. We found a village called Arnekati (Arne is 'elephant'), where half the people are a tribe and half newcomers to the village. We had to walk the last bit of the path from this village to the house because the road was too steep for the vehicle and badly formed. We first came to the mother's workplace, which was a large coffee farm, but they also grew cardamom, peppercorns, ginger, chillis, dhal, and tea. There were more wonderful flowering trees and roses and spectacular views. The other

106

people living in this road were thrilled to see us - I don't really know why - and at one house we were given bananas and freshly squeezed limejuice. At another home we had coffee ground from their own beans in a huge grinder sitting in the corner of the kitchen. We stopped and talked to everyone along the road between the farm and the little boy's house. Sunbeam translated all the things I wanted to know. Everyone *wanted* to talk and I was absolutely spellbound by all they had to say, and they were so curious about my circumstances and life in England. I didn't even laugh until afterwards about the actively amorous goats doing 'it' within inches of us while we talked on their doorstep.

The lovely little 'last boy' was called Samvel Samuel but they pronounced their 'u's as 'v's. He waved goodbye to his mum, quite happily, but Mary said he would probably be sad in a couple of days' time. The ones that were sad at first were happy after two days, and the initially happy ones have a bit of reaction after a couple of days. They certainly all appeared to me to settle within a week and didn't seem to need my carefully planned Buddy System since *all* the other boys become their Buddy immediately. Clutching a huge Jackfruit, presented to us by one of his neighbours, we left for home. This Jackfruit looked like an enormous marrow, but was definitely a *fruit* with a distinctive flavour. In a village on the way home, Sunbeam, Mani the driver, and I shared bottles of Pepsi, two slices of heavenly coconut puff, two vegetable puffs in the best pastry I've ever had, and a cup of tea, and it all came to the equivalent of 33 pence.

The temperature was divine and I was certainly in no hurry to return to the town but I soon started enjoying the funny town things again. For instance a rickshaw taxi passed us that was full of goats which were held in by their owner, and a tall, beautiful woman walked past us with raggle/taggle hair in which nestled a newspaper parcel tied up with twine. There was a sign at one corner of the street, saying 'Safety Saves Lives' and another announcing that 'We The Old Book Shop Have Shifted to Old Road'.

When I got home, the first person I met was the sweeper lady to whom I had donated some Tesco tomato puree, which I didn't need. She complained about it, in mime, and demonstrated that she had thought it was toothpaste.

Back at the office there had been a minor (!) drama. One of the girls had been given an injection by Raji to 'calm her down'. When I queried this, Raji told me that the girl had said that she didn't want to live with us anymore. Her mother had got very cross and insisted that the girl must stay, whereupon she had become 'His Treacle' Raji's translation of the word hysterical - so what could she do?

The Rains continued for days. It was a completely different country - in the wet. Most days someone would inform me that this was the last day of it but every morning, there it was gently bucketing down. There were huge puddles everywhere and hundreds of very droopy Indians. They predictably hated the cold and wet and the Orphanage doctor solemnly informed me that the children must only bathe - buckets of water thrown over themselves - on alternate days. He insisted they must have their drinks and food heated until the warmer weather returned. (He didn't seem to have any suggestions about improving the bedding situation so they were all still sleeping on rush mats on concrete, with virtually no blankets to cover them). He definitely would NOT have approved of Pointy Ears and I skipping about and splashing each other in an enormous puddle outside my house yesterday. It was such *fun* because it was a *warm* puddle.

Everything had rapidly gone mouldy, though, in the hot and wet. Can you imagine the problem of drying the washing for 500 children? It just got smellier and smellier. I looked forward to the return of the hellfire heat. Another problem was the seven or eight boys lying on mats with 'fever' at any one time and *loads* of runny noses, too.

However, two boys - Udyhakumar and Jaffierelli or Jaffa, as he was called - wanted to ignore the rain and go to town with me, on the bus, for a treat. They were eagerly waiting for me at the gate. Udyhakumar had a luminous pink towel wrapped round his head and Jaffa - sixteen years old and very decidedly eccentric - chose a green towel. What with their colourful accessories and 'Mummy' looking like a greenish-skinned, female Gulliver and carrying a black umbrella with gold stars inside - the stares of the natives were pretty justified. Anyway the people *didn't* smile at us today but Jaffa, who hadn't been to town for years - more than made up for them. The situation just struck me so funny. I knew that the reason Jaffa hadn't been to town for years was the other boys' embarrassment at his strange appearance and the involuntary loud noises that he made. (I have wondered since if he had Tourette's syndrome, but I couldn't tell if he was swearing when he shouted out in Tamil!). He couldn't cope with school and was always at the gate of the Boys' House when I called. I always shouted "Narlaki" - meaning 'Tomorrow' - every time he grabbed my arm and asked to go out with me, but I relented on this miserable day and his joy made it all worth while.

Although his behaviour certainly didn't detract from our enjoyment of this bizarre expedition, I could see that it would have been agony for the other boys. It made an interesting little item to include on his Report, which I typed that week. I reported on every child for the sponsors, using the Volunteers' typewriter in my house. This was an annual requirement for the charity. I did a few words of description of each boy's progress, their height, weight, medical history for the year and, if it was interesting, anything which had particularly pleased or distressed them. A Tamil speaker usually typed the reports, in English, so I hoped my efforts weren't too pathetic by comparison. They didn't have anyone to translate this year, so I devised a sort of chart with the questions along the top and tick boxes for me to fill in when the children answered. Sunbeam seemed very relieved at my speedy solution to this annual chore, and the children *loved* the attention the questionnaire drew. They *helped* each other with replies to the questions and I wished I could spend longer on all of them, they were so delightfully pleased with their lives and content to be in such a large 'family'.

A little wild, white cat visited me most days and was definitely a mixed blessing in my house. She often upset the milk, if I had accidentally left it out after the girls delivered it for me each night. She upset it at 2 a.m., one night, all over the floor, and of course it was when the electricity had cut out. I think I must have been upsetting him/her psychologically because half of me wanted her to visit me to keep the rats out and look pretty, and the other half didn't want her because she even scratched her way into ant-proof packets of crisps and sweets. She hung from the outside windowsill, one day, looking in the window with her head between her two front paws. When she saw me, just her head sunk out of view slowly, leaving only her paws visible. It was so funny and she reminded me of my grandson - she was just going to be naughty but then thought better of it.

A second invasion of nits arrived and so I decided one day to have my hair cut. The Orphanage barber was very good with the little boys' hair so I was a bit amazed at what he did for me. He appeared to understand my demonstration of what and where to cut. I must say though, I looked like one of those animated vegetables in children's books and I made up my mind not to have cut it again until I got home. While he was cutting it, one of the many girls watching started to cry, and another muttered something about Michael Jackson, so I should've known what to expect. I joked about having a manicure as well, spreading my hands out to demonstrate, and the supervisor went for the nail cutters that they cut the boys' nails with and offered to oblige. I had to be so careful with flippant remarks because most of the time my English brand of humour fell on serious, caring and thoughtful ears, here, and got lost.

The Exhibition ran for ages in town and the staff wanted to take some more of the children to it. Apart from the fact that the girls hadn't been at all yet, there was a stall for the 'craft' which children and staff had made during the year to raise funds. The teachers wanted to see their objects on sale. Well, the Special Girls and their teacher wanted *me* to take them and I added seven of my boys to the party and we had a riotous day together. Some of us went on the bus and I explained about the purchase of the tickets to Rani, a Special girl sitting next to me. I gave her the tickets given to me for all the children and then the change from the ticket collector but she promptly popped the money into her mouth! I was trying to extract it, holding her head under my arm, with at least 80 people (honestly!) watching me. Her teeth looked like those orange peel ones you make, and were absolutely clamped shut.

When we got to the park, the biggest girl, Raina, kept lunging at me to give me a bear hug and I kept falling over because she never did it when I expected her to. Another girl kept removing her knickers altogether and her friend kept storing food up the leg of hers. She had this huge bulge on one side and it was full of pappadoms, and battered deep-fried chillis. We sat on huge expanses of coconut matting provided for the Indian families to picnic on. It was great fun but of course the Special Girls kept moving off the mat when we weren't looking. This was mostly when *I* was left in charge. They kept plonking themselves down in the middle of other family parties. The Indians were intrigued with these weird girls and kept giving them food and staring and staring at them. I enjoyed this, in a way, because on previous expeditions there had been only ME as the star attraction. The boys, of course, did their best to be sitting away from us all and got very tired of explaining what *I* was doing there, as well as excusing the girls' actions.

111

During this expedition, a mosquito drilled a hole in me, underneath my watch. I was so pleased that they were not the malarial kind in this part of India. I freaked about my room, one day, trying to get one out of the inside of my dress, but realised it was just sweat trickling down and not a mosquito at all. The bites and the itching are bearable, but when they go septic they are horrible and take ages to heal up.

The Event of one weekend for us was another visit of the Church Youth Group. Four or five earnest youngsters, about 20 years old, came with a load of speakers and a keyboard and let the children dance and sing with them - they loved it. Of course they requested a song from *me* but I didn't know any. The only way I could compensate for being such a failure was to promise to write all about my role in the Orphanage for their church Newsletter. They appeared satisfied with this idea as my return contribution for their successful visit. There were about 300 children in a very small room and they clapped and smiled and loved every minute. Even the Special Boys were allowed to dance on the stage - to their huge delight. They had negotiated a very 'hairy' walk to the hall from their house - mingling with buffalo, motorbikes and demented bus drivers. We had walked in a 'crocodile', pushing the two rusty old wheelchairs as well and it was awful but the Church Youth Group's enthusiasm and 'musicality' were well worth the effort. I had distributed consolation gift balloons to the Special boys left behind because they were bed bound and to the ones whose 'insides come out, Mummy!' the incontinent boys - but I made up my mind to persuade the Church Youth boys to 'do a gig' in our compound another time, so that they could all join in.

CHAPTER THIRTEEN

About Nurse Edith and her family and an action-packed trip to Kathmandu.

Edith was an Anglo-Indian Night Nurse who lived at the bottom of my road. She was 67 years old, but only looked 45. She invited me to supper and let me watch her cook it, write down the recipes, and see all the different spices and herbs she used. Her husband had had a stroke and I think probably had Alzheimer's Disease as well. His speech was badly impaired but he was a historian and wanted to discuss Thomas Becket and other English historical figures, so I did my best. His wife and daughters made no secret of the fact that his running out in the road with no clothes on, losing track of what was day and what was night and other similar incidents, left them frazzled and impatient with him. I was happy to talk to such an intelligent man - he was having a good day - and kept him entertained for a couple of hours, to their enormous relief. They said having company in their house was usually difficult, because of his unpredictability, and only their religious meetings were possible, when the small congregation knew all the problems.

On the evening they invited me to supper, I enjoyed dressing up, buying flowers to take to them and of course seeing their lovely house and meeting the two daughters for the first time. One of them was a student at the University, and the other an Army Major. I promised to send to England to try and get a replacement of an essential piece of Edith's precious pressure cooker, which was broken. A German volunteer had given it to her, years ago, and she loved it and said it was much better than Indian-grown pressure cookers. The family were ardently involved in the Church of South India religion and had regular services and hymn singing in their home. I learned that they confess their sins as the Roman Catholics do, but they confess them to Jesus, not a Minister of their Church. They hoped that I would join them for this one evening while I was staying, and promised that there was a lot of *singing* which I would love.

Edith made curried madavar for supper. It was chopped onion and tomatoes, fried with balls of coriander powder, garlic and ginger ground together, using a stone. She added more curry powder and water and salt and simmered it for fifteen minutes and then added ground coconut and vinegar and water and dropped this madavar fish into the sauce and simmered another fifteen minutes.

Edith didn't mind me examining and questioning her about cooking and Indian food generally and seemed proud to instruct me. I felt really sorry for her in so many ways. Their life was so difficult, especially because of the father's ailments, and the younger daughter wanted to leave home to live near the University, but was anxious about going away while her mother was having such a hard time. The elder girl was badly affected by that hereditary skin complaint that makes brown and white pigment come out all over your face and hands. She was having a very successful career in the Army but was very distressed when this problem with her skin suddenly appeared. I asked another nurse in India what the name of that complaint was, and she said, "Patches, Mummy," as if to say, "What else?"

Another English-speaking Indian friend didn't live nearby, but she taught the boys next door, every day, and came to visit me at some time most days. She told me that her husband knocked her about because he was depressed. She was the breadwinner as he couldn't get a job - he was a milkman. She had been so badly treated by him that she called on her Church people (Elim Pentecostal) - to have a word with him. They did. She told me the next month that she was pregnant again.

Emily, a lovely neighbour of mine in England, visited with her new husband, a Sudanese boy called Hassim. They arrived in Coimbatore and I met them at the railway station while taking some boys on their maiden voyage on a train. I had been taking parties of boys on the train from Podanur to Combatoire because they live at this important rail junction and had never experienced rail journeys. Emily walked right past me on the station. She simply didn't recognise me because I had no hair to speak of, and looked thin and green complexioned. We had a noisy, emotional re-union on the station and then they helped me take the boys over the very busy roads to the café we always visited, for Pepsi and buns. (They have to only drink a half a bottle each because it blows them right up, and one bun lasts ages.) It was certainly a good introduction to the boys for Emily and Hassim. There were three who are deaf and dumb, assorted boys on crutches, several boys carrying each other and one lengthy, thin boy that I carried up and downstairs, in the station, to their huge amusement.

Hassim was wearing a big, multi-coloured, knitted hat over his dreadlocks and this - and the mixed marriage - caused enormous interest everywhere we went. He was sweet-natured man but he got very tired of the attention and was particularly upset when a man in a slowly passing train snatched at his hat. He said there were fewer hassles in Podanur than in Hyderabad, where they had been recently. I couldn't find anywhere for them to stay in our village so they took the train back to town each night.

It was wonderful for me to talk and talk and talk to Emily about our friends and family in England. She had thoughtfully bought me the Lonely Planet Guide to Nepal which I had walked miles searching for in India, ever since I had decided to visit Kathmandu. (This wonderful book even gave me the Poste Restante address for while I was there). They had known of these publications before they went to India, and found the Indian version full of interesting and vital statistics and information, and had guessed that I would benefit from the Nepal version.

Emily and Hassim lived in a thatched home on the beach in a fishing village in Goa. They hadn't been there long, and it was lovely to be able to pass on to her various kitchen items and bed linen, which I would not need for much longer. Hassim met up with some other Muslim men in the village and was welcomed and taken to their homes. There weren't many Muslims in Podanur (that I knew of anyway) but I heard a lot of bell ringing from a Mosque near me which I never saw. I learnt from one of my women friends that Hindu men wishing to get rid of their wives could convert to the Muslim faith and take second or third wives. They only had to say they didn't want their first wife and she had to go. He could have four wives if he could support them but he is bound to treat them equally. Muslim women and men eat separately and everyone prays five times daily from the age of seven onwards. A visit to Mecca is everyone's aim in life. While his new friends entertained Hassim, Emily and I gossiped about home and talked to the boys and girls in the Orphanage. Then - best of all - they both helped me to take a photograph of every child to send to their Sponsors in England and Canada. I had been worrying about using the new camera, which had been donated for the purpose, because it was very sophisticated. Emily and Hassim knew all about the lenses and focuses and all those technical things, and so I just arranged the kids with their Orphanage numbers in front of them, and they clicked away, and we raced through the job. It was good fun, instead of a sweaty problem. I was sad to see them go, and I missed them, but it had been a real treat to have them to stay, and I know they enjoyed their visit and the insight into the workings of an orphanage, very much.

116

Everyone in the Orphanage was interested in my trip to Kathmandu, which was necessary, as I wanted to renew my visa for being in India for another six months. I was only allowed a six months visa when I left England but I had been told by the Madras Embassy that it would be no problem to obtain another six months, if I applied for it in Kathmandu. They said I had to leave India to renew it, and I decided that Nepal would be a better idea than Sri Lanka, where there was currently some terrorist trouble.

At 6.45 a.m. on the day I left, Edith bought me some mutton stew for my 'tiffin' (breakfast), plus a picture of herself when she was a girl (1930) and some Revival Hymn tapes.

I called in the Office on the way to the station, to telephone the Bank in town to plead for news of my Visa card, which had again been withdrawn for unknown reasons. The negative reply on the 'phone, and waiting time while they made enquiries, weren't helped by the rendering of Happy Birthday to You which was played constantly while I waited. I borrowed some rupees from Mr. Suami, the Accountant, to tide me over in Nepal and vowed to change Banks on my return from Kathmandu.

While walking in heavy rain to the station I met the Clerk, Mr. Suami's brother, going to the Office on his bicycle. He was an amazing sight, swathed in luminous pink plastic garments and topped with an emerald green, woollen pixie hood! He was followed by a man taking his cockerel for a walk down the road on a pink ribbon lead. India was never boring.

All Aboard the Mandala Mail Train. The journey from Coimbatore to Delhi was going to take 48 hours and I had happily agreed to Indira's request to accompany me to see what travelling without a man was like. Indira was interested in women's problems in India and worked hard to encourage them to improve their lot. She arranged our tickets for the trip to Kathmandu, and we would travel about 2,500 miles through India. The train fare was only £28 one way, and we had a two-people compartment to sleep in. I wore my best salwar khameez and she, of course, wore yet another beautiful sari. We drew even more curious glances than usual from the public as we searched for our carriage. Indira's son accompanied us in this and was able to make sense of the lists of passengers printed on the carriages - I would certainly never have found ours. I got the strongest feeling that he wasn't absolutely delighted about his mother going off with a solitary Englishwoman and I couldn't help contrasting his reserve with the teasing, light-hearted attitude that my similar-aged son would have had in these circumstances. His mother was keen to experience travelling without her family and to see India through a foreigner's eyes. I think she only half-believed the anecdotes I had told her about the harassment from Indian men, and endured by single Western women and this trip certainly opened her eyes.

However, no sooner had we installed ourselves comfortably, washed our 'smalls' and hung them to dry, and ordered our meal, than a weedy youth came into the carriage. He asked if we would let his frail, elderly mother sleep on our floor. Indira was all for refusing but I couldn't. Anyway he went off and returned with this huge woman, at least ten years younger than me, and helped her settle herself and her bags on our floor. After he left us - to stand up all night, I suppose, she bought out her personal symbol of the God, Lord Krishna, which she kept in a sandwich box. She showed him to us, lit her incense, prayed and then said, "I'll let him sleep, now". She suggested we say goodnight to him, which we dutifully did, and she returned him to his box and then she lay down on our floor and went to sleep.

There was a loo/shower/sink arrangement at the end of the corridor and we found that there was a regular time of day when it was cleaned properly and we could use it happily. The tea and coffee (both sugary but piping hot) were supplied cheaply and regularly, as were the good meals delivered on stainless steel trays and the time passed pleasantly, watching India go past the windows.

In Bhopal (the belly button of India I was told, and where there had been a ghastly chemical plant disaster), I was excited to see tea being sold in small pottery tea bowls on the platform. I knew these would interest my son, Leigh, who is a potter. Indira encouraged me to go and get a couple as the tea is sold *with* the bowl, so I jumped out. However, when she saw me go past our window she screamed, "Come, Jenny - Fast!" And her eyes were like halves of hard-boiled eggs. I then realised the train was silently gliding away from the station. I raced along and jumped back on the train, up a very high step. I had to grab the handles and throw myself in the door and on to the floor of the carriage like an enormous sack of potatoes, much to the amazement of hoards of onlookers, in and out of the train.

It was so funny. But of course it wouldn't have been amusing if I'd been left on the platform, because we were in the middle of India and I had no money, ticket, passport or even Pictures of the Grandchildren with me. Indira thought I knew that you just call out to the tea-bowl sellers from the train doorway.

Even before this somewhat unusual incident, the people on the train were fascinated at the sight of an Englishwoman, travelling alone. "Are you an English Eccentric?" I was asked. One man hit his head on the doorjamb as he passed my carriage - he was so busy peering in at me. We were met in Delhi by Indira's friend, Mr. Singh the Bank Manager, and his driver, who took us to our hotel. There was an ensuite shower in our room and a television showing the Wimbledon Tennis Tournament! Indira didn't share my delight in watching this wonderful English treat, but she settled swiftly and contentedly on her bed in something like the lotus position and meditated - on the weird passions of the English, perhaps? The room and shower were less than clean by our standards and the electricity supply was by means of plugs and wires that looked like a cartoon, but we were two very happy women for a couple of hours. I had diced with death to get the television working via the frayed, electric wires and foreign plugs but the tennis matches were well worth the risk. The bright green and red parrots outside the windows, perched in tangled branches of a jacaranda tree, competed for my attention, and were an exotic bonus for me.

I recommended the American Nerula's Restaurant that I knew of, to my companions, for our supper. I had been told of it by Heather, and they were very impressed. Mr. Singh had never used knife, fork and spoon before but he managed very well and was amused to try. They were particularly fascinated when I demonstrated loading food on the *back* of the fork and I was glad I hadn't chosen peas for my supper. Mr. Singh was scandalised by Indira drinking beer with me and his big grin was the very reaction Indira wished for.

They took me to a Son et Lumiere in Red Fort, Delhi, after supper. The time it would start was a bit of a problem because they didn't know 'when blackness was coming' and the notices only gave this clue to the official starting time. There were wonderful coloured lights and very loud, refined British voices on the Tannoy system, describing the history of Red Fort. There were even the sounds of tramping British soldiers and it was very realistic and frightening, really. There were multitudes of mosquitoes biting us throughout the whole production but it didn't spoil our enjoyment of what was excellent entertainment. Happily the scandalous facts revealed about the British actions in the past didn't seem to affect Indira and Mr. Singh's affection for me.

The next day, Indira and I went on a tourist bus round Delhi, which included a visit to Indira Ghandi's home. We saw her study and memorabilia, including her spectacles and Scrabble set. We were shown the exact spot on which she died in her garden. There were also numerous photographs of the rest of the Ghandi family and of the English Royal Family, and newspapers displayed everywhere that were relevant to the War and the assassinations. I could have stayed for days, it was so interesting. This visit, and the shopping in Red Fort, were particularly pleasant for me in Indira's company. She answered all the things I needed to know and coped with the problems that would've upset me, had I been on my own. For instance, there were beggars everywhere and one particular boy with a baby in his arms and a younger still girl with a baby, too, were pretty upsetting. There was also a little boy with a Charlie Chaplin moustache painted on him, and he did handstands and a funny walk, to try to get money for food. You think you can cope with these sights but every now and again something triggers you off, and you cry with pity and frustration. Indira was less ambivalent about the numerous 'Anglophiles', who ignored *her* and only talked to *me*, while we were on the tourist route. She found this particularly aggravating, but didn't let it spoil our day - though she sulked a bit when one woman was asking me questions about which Indira had more knowledge than me.

The flight to Kathmandu (about £45, with £3 airport tax) was delayed an hour but we enjoyed the free refreshments we were offered and talked to a man travelling from Graz, Austria - mostly on his bike. On arrival in Kathmandu, I didn't have the necessary American dollars to buy my visa for Nepal (£14) so I had to leave my passport at the airport and collect it the next day. I waited a good hour in a queue of American incoming tourists, to get it back and then the officials said they'd lost it. I pretended to cry (not difficult - I was desperate) and it was found and returned to me quite quickly after this. Someone told me after that I could've got it even more speedily if I had offered money, and that it probably was not lost at all.

Indira and I visited a couple of towns and several temples, around Kathmandu and found Nepal to be a very colourful and exciting country. We sat outside a café and drank a beer and felt very decadent - it would very definitely not be approved of in our 'home' town in India. It was only when I went on a trip away from the village that I was conscious of how much I was being careful to preserve the niceties in India. I had been alarmed to learn that a Volunteer at our Orphanage was once 'repatriated' in a hurry because she had leapt on an elephant's back during a festival. She had got carried away (!) by the excitement of the procession and had jumped up on the elephant. The fact that she had her legs apart was sufficiently wicked to cause her to be sent home by the Western officers - not the Indians - I was interested to learn.

Much to her disgust, Indira had attracted an admirer on the 'plane and he had found out her telephone number at the Hotel. He kept ringing her up and I explained to her that this was just one of the disadvantages of travelling on your own, and nothing to worry about. The hotel we found was called the Two Seater Rest House - or something like that - and they served pots of tea, or coffee in a teapot, for 50p. so I knew I would like it there. (Four nights for two and meals for one were £28). My first Nepalese meal was green peppers and chicken in curry sauce in a 'jungle garden' in this hotel. Indira had crashed out with fatigue so I ate alone but it was nevertheless a lovely evening. The courtyard garden was full of exotic foliage and flowers and the humidity and noise of temple bells and traffic gave me such pleasure. I didn't even feel the need to *read* which I usually like to do if I am alone in a restaurant. In the bathroom there was a full sized tree growing up through the roof and mushrooms growing at its' base. Very wonderful to look at but I did notice my clothes were also damp enough to grow mushrooms on, after only one night. Kathmandu was thick with exhaust fumes but just as exciting and 'eventful' to walk about in, as India. A pickup truck passed us one day with the open back full of the softest Wedgwood-blue knitting wool, unwrapped; a boy crashed into a taxi and hauled the driver off to the nearby cycle repair shop to get an estimate for repair, accompanied by 20 or 25

Nepalese witnesses and advisers. While I waited for Indira to visit a Hindu temple that didn't allow Christian visitors, I talked to a man about a leprosy hospital run by three Americans, next door to the temple; I also met a nurse called Bridget who worked with Medicines Sans Frontiers in Tibet. She was having a holiday break from her pretty hectic life there and from her account of her work she had certainly earned a rest.

The Chaps at the Embassy were adamant about there being no possibility of getting my visa in under a week. The Madras Office had misinformed me. I was appalled because I had very little money with me and my credit card had been confiscated in India. I showed the Indians in the Visa Office my flight ticket, a reference letter from Orphanage and even the Pictures of my Grandchildren, but to no avail. They were all rude and horrible to me and to countless Americans and Japanese who were crying and pleading through the little grill high up on the Embassy wall. The officials said things like:

"Why do you think you can treat India so cheaply, thinking you can come and go as you wish?"

"Can't you read? It says write in *black* pen!"

"Can't you write more clearly?"

"Stop that (crying) immediately!"

"Why are you travelling alone?"

"What is your husband thinking of, that he would allow you to allow you to travel singly?"

There was another English girl waiting, who I thought very brave when she replied to this last question: "I am on a mission from God!" That shut him up for a while. I wish I had thought to say: "I couldn't find anyone else daft enough to come to India". (Perhaps not)

There was nowhere to fill in their wretched forms and you had to do all the negotiating through a vent too high up for me to see through. It seemed to be either pouring with rain or boiling hot every time I went there. I went several times and in the end resigned myself to waiting eight days in the hotel with no money, eating bananas because they were cheap. They said I could only have a three months visa, too, and not six months, as I wished. I was so disappointed because I had promised the boys I would 'do' an English Christmas.

The British Embassy staff, in the office nearby, were lovely, but said they couldn't help as even their own staff couldn't get a visa in less than five days. They were pleasant and sympathetic and even had a notice on their wall saying you must allow one and a half days to obtain a visa for Britain.

I *did* allow myself a cheap breakfast from time to time, in the jungle garden, with incense burning and many strange birds singing. I read the first news from England since I had left home, in the English-language Nepali papers in the hotel. Accounts of John Major's alleged girlfriend and Lady Di's divorce arrangements seemed so unreal.

Indira urged me to write letters of complaint about the Embassy, with copies to everyone else in the world. She was quite calm about having to return to Coimbatore without me, and it would be an opportunity to really see what travelling singly was like.

Twelve days after leaving the Orphanage, I got the visa! I showed the Pictures of Grandchildren to the Duty Officer at 9.00 a.m. on the day I had been told to call - and shamelessly 'licked his boots' by admiring *his* Pictures of Grandchildren. I returned, as instructed, at 4.30 p.m. and there was my Visa. It was, however, only valid for three months and I was so depressed about the fact that I would not be at the Orphanage for Christmas that I told the Nepalese waiter in the hotel about my disappointment. He just looked at my crumpled face and suggested that if India didn't want me to look after their little boys, why didn't I come back and look after *their* little boys for three months?

I had, coincidentally, called to see a Nepalese Orphanage up the road from the hotel, the day before. I had only called in to see if I could pick up some tips and see how their children were cared for, really, but I had liked what I saw and returned that very day to see if they would like a helper in September. They said they would, but could not provide accommodation or pay. It certainly gave me something to think about, anyway, and it alleviated my initial disappointment about leaving Podanur early.

Indira had to return earlier than I, but I had met another girl called Heather, at the Indian Embassy, who ran a Scuba Diving School in Lanzarotti. She was travelling all over the World and was also trying to extend her visa. She was tiny, with blonde, long, curly hair and she had got very tired of the sexual harassment in Kathmandu while she waited. She told me she had been to most countries in the world, on her own, and Nepal was the worst place for *men*. As far as places to visit - she favoured Australia even though 'they have the worst bed bugs'. She thought she'd like to be a Jillaroo there, working on a cattle station. It sounded the worst job I'd ever heard of watching horns and whatnots being removed. She told me she had a Sloany sister, and parents living in Edinburgh, and her marriage had faltered (for the same reason as Nancy's I think) so she had come away to have adventures. She said she would be 40 on 12th August and might come and see me at the Orphanage to celebrate it! Meanwhile we celebrated the receipt of our Visas to return to India, with pots of tea in the jungly garden of my hotel.

My flight back to Delhi was delayed by two hours and this time all the passengers were taken to a wonderful hotel called The Everest. Lunch was five choices of wonderful things like fish curry or vegetable lasagne. There were at least five waiters, waiting to see what we desired and there were lovely thick white napkins and heavy cutlery and the company was fantastic. At my table I met a crazy interior designer called Gail from New York, who told me her

125

current project was to turn a shop into a huge chocolate box in which to sell hand-made chocolates. There was a psychologist from South Africa called Larrice, and an Australian father and daughter - she was a music student and he was a rather 'British style' businessman. The pair of them appeared to have fallen out rather badly. Lastly there was a sweet little Nepali businessman, who availed himself of my emergency sticking plasters for a cut finger, which was bleeding over his nice suit. (My Emergency Medical Kit still only held sticking plasters and aspirin but I hadn't needed anything else more drastic and other people were still only requesting these two things.)

On the flight I sat next to a darling Indian man whose 16 year old daughter had died of heart trouble. He ordered beer and chicken curry for me but I was feeling so overfed by now - what with the lovely meal in the hotel and after my limited diet in Kathmandu - that I didn't do it justice.

I was reading 'City of Joy' the nitty gritty about Calcutta, and this saw me through a rather boring night in the Palace Heights Hotel in Delhi, where Raji and I had experienced our somewhat traumatic night earlier in the year. It was still less than lovely but it was in an area that I could find without too much trouble so I went there from necessity. Before bed I had a walk around the streets near the hotel and found a coffee house where they played '20s music on a grand piano, and made me tea with separate milk. On my return to the hotel, I noticed a little family sleeping on the road just a short distance from the window of my room. They were part of a group of assorted men, women and children sleeping outside and when I looked out a couple of times during the night and early morning, the little boy of the family was the only one awake and he just sat, playing perfectly quietly under the stars.

The night was very sticky and my bed somewhat unsavoury but I found the train station without too much trouble in the morning, so I didn't regret choosing that hotel. The Coimbatore train from Delhi went from Hazrat

126

Mizamuddin Station, which I had not been in before. I had a row with the auto-rickshaw man when I paid him but I'd just had a restorative breakfast of fresh orange, best coffee and a tomato and bacon omelette in Nerula's so I was in good spirits and didn't let him upset me. When searching for my carriage in the train, a newly ordained Roman Catholic priest happened along and guided me to my place. A qualified Shepherd caring for his first sheep, I wondered. Leaving Delhi at 10.00 a.m. with three, initially miserable, Indian men in the four people sleeper, I once more watched India flow past the window for two days and never got bored. There were paddy fields, thatched sheds, factories, buffalo, goats, pigs, elephants, Roman Catholic mission schools, the Taj Mahal in the distance at Agra, Goldfield Public School (the same name as my granddaughter's school in England), egrets, buzzards, black hairy pigs, camels eating a hedge, kilns made of the bricks which *made* the bricks, Bhopal, people cleaning their teeth with acacia twigs instead of brushes, people sleeping on the platforms, families having picnics while they waited for trains. It was absolutely fascinating.

Meanwhile, 'The Lads' in my carriage bucked up after we had all showered and one of them, called Rao, (a very handsome military policeman) got out some rum and the Bombay mix. We waited for our dinners to be delivered after *they* ordered what they thought I should have. The dinners arrived on stainless steel trays again and comprised delicious hot spicy things and rice in compartments, like a T.V. Dinner. 'Ovaries' (or something like that) was an engineer with a bad back, about 37 years old, and 'Rumour', was a retired gent, who left the carriage most of the time because he couldn't bear hearing me talk English (He didn't know he is not alone in the World). They were all very good company and we swapped recipes and talked about English and Indian education systems, and Life.

Rao had to pay a huge fine to a skeletal, miserable official, for having excess luggage, which was weighed in the train by a Charlie Drake lookalike, using some balance scales. I asked him what was in the big parcels but he either didn't understand, or didn't want to tell me what it was.

Ovaries was very shy but got quite animated talking about food. His favourite recipe was any vegetable, coated in wheat powder and egg and deep-fried until tender. Rao loved Samba which is vegetables with garam masala and samba powder (don't know what that is exactly) plus dhal. They told me that cardamom is very good for the digestion. I loved how Indians always entreated you to "fry it nicely" and I imagined their appropriately righteous faces while they cooked.

Rao smoked tiny little cigarettes called bidis and they smelled so Indian to me, that I wished I liked to smoke. He was the first Indian I had actually talked to that smoked - hardly anyone seemed to.

I clambered, somewhat inelegantly and self-consciously up to my shelf-bed but the motion of the train and a bit of fatigue ensured a really good night's sleep. Next morning The Lads all slept during the day as well, but I couldn't stop looking out of the window, eating or talking to other people. After my egg curry breakfast and endless sugared coffee I found a couple in another carriage that wanted to talk philosophy. They thought my visit here was predestined because of something to do with my Uncle Robert from Ireland. The husband suggested I might be in India to be rewarded for *his* efforts in India but the wife thought I was probably meant to serve the children in India to thank the Indians for their efforts in 'our' War.

A man looked into our carriage one day and asked, "What is your native country?" which is a very common conversation starter here. I was going to launch into my life history as usual when Rao suddenly leapt to his feet and booted the man up the corridor. He said the man was a thief. I thought Rao was just being a macho policeman and thanked him but assured him that men often use that enquiry as an excuse to talk English or even just to talk to a

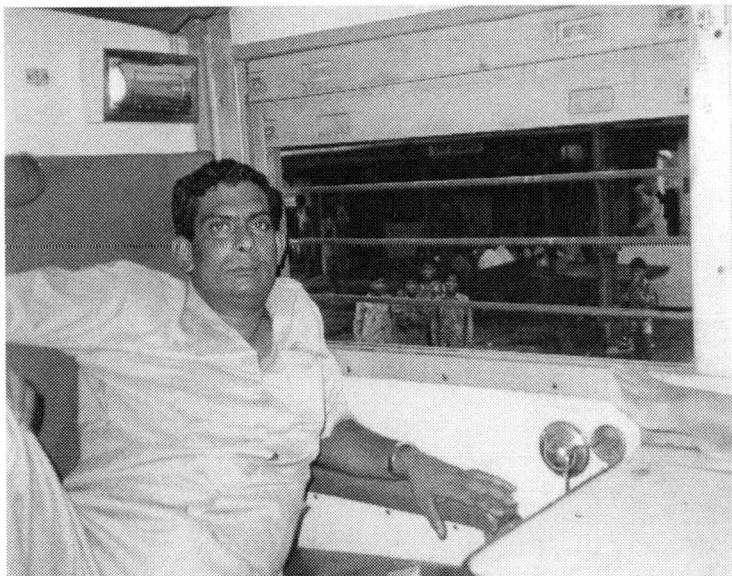

Rao, the Indian Casanova

Western woman. He obviously didn't agree with me, though, and sulked for a while.

Rao was proved right the next morning, though, when the communication cord was pulled somewhere and he called me to look out of the window. I saw the railway police marching the thief - for so he was - away from the train, Rao said he knew the man was a thief from the way his eyes had darted about the carriage looking at where my luggage was positioned, and planning how he would remove it.

I spent quite a lot of time talking to the men about the way Western women are perceived in India. Because of the nature of the films shown in India, and the posters and magazine articles about them, it is assumed that we are all immoral. The posters all showed white women laid back in scant undies, eating bananas or pouting. The posters were usually about thirty feet tall and I was so embarrassed about them when my small boys pointed them out to me. I explained to my fellow passengers - and anyone else in India who would listen - that we weren't 'like that' at all. I thought I had been pretty eloquent on this occasion, but at five a.m. one morning - Rao climbed up to my bunk and tried to get in with me. I banged my fist on his hand on the top rung of the bunk bed ladder. He laughed and got down again in a hurry, nursing what might have been a broken hand. I didn't feel menaced at all but *honestly!* . He spoke English and Hindi and I couldn't understand either of his spoken languages very well but I *could* understand his big brown eyes, and he definitely wanted me to get out with him at his stop.

I thought a lot about all this, afterwards, and I suppose I can understand these assumptions about us because Indians must see us as willing casual partners because of our contraceptives, divorces, liberated life-styles and the way we travel about on our own. This is so different to their 'ownership' of their women and indeed the women's acceptance of dependence on men. (What *really* amazed me about 'the incident' was *my own* palpitating exhilaration and pleasure when he stroked my arm and looked at me *like that* in the dimly lit carriage!)

Rao and the retired gent got out one night earlier than Ovaries and I, but I wasn't worried about sleeping alone with him - because he had a bad back, you understand - and wasn't either romantic or menacing. The remainder of the journey was pleasantly uneventful and I started to look forward to seeing the boys again and to settling back into my little Indian home.

I enjoyed some idlis - vegetarian snacks - offered at the window of the train. I needed a bit of advice from Ovaries to negotiate the price and select the goods before the train took off again. I certainly knew not to get *out of* the train, after my adventure at Bhopal.

I treated myself to an auto-rickshaw from the Podanur station to the Orphanage, and I was overjoyed to collect a huge pile of post from the Office on the way home. I made several heavenly pots of *unsugared* tea to drink while I revelled in news from friends and relations.

It was back to work with a vengeance after this break in Nepal and I began to think I must start to say a firm No to a few requests from staff to do things. This plan was partly to preserve my, so far, good health and strength. The women often said, "Aren't you *paining* anywhere, Mummy?" because I could walk and work so much longer than they could - and did. I suppose it is our superior diet and medication from birth that gives me the edge on them for stamina. I am also strongly of the opinion that we are workaholics - compared to Indians. I took months to stop watching my watch, and feeling guilty if I took both feet off the ground *during the day!* It was because of my reputation for non-stop work, that I was requested to do things *all the time* and I found it hard to refuse.

CHAPTER FOURTEEN

A Communion Service, a trip to Mysore, a Sports Day and an unsuccessful yoga session.

On the first day back from Kathmandu, I photographed some girls, took an English class at Girls' House which is a half mile walk there and back, took 10 boys on the train to Coimbatore and had Pepsis and buns and got the train back. In the evening I went to another Prayer Meeting. There was the usual hand clapping and Alleluja-ing, and I was on the point of agreeing to their request that I inspect a new, life-sized Virgin Mary statue, which had been erected in the village, while I was away. However, I thought better of it and declined the invitation and went home and fell in a heap. This 'Mary' had been very firmly constructed at the crossroads in a sort of concrete telephone box shrine and was pretty amazing really. I have nothing against Mary, but I couldn't help feeling the money and effort would have been more usefully spent on a concrete bus shelter on that spot, with seats, and protection from the grilling sun, for the villagers. This wasn't the reason I declined the invitation to go with them to admire her, but I felt so guilty saying I was too tired to go, even though in that instance, *I was*.

When I collected the boys for another trip to the zoo one day, they were all being smothered in talcum powder to make them look lighter-skinned! It made them look like little clowns in my eyes, but I just had to admire their clean clothes and keep quiet about the talc. Another colourful addition to their appearance was their scabies 'cure', which involved loads of gentian violet being spread on them. I knew it didn't solve the problem and it made them look frightful but I could not dissuade the Orphanage doctor from prescribing it. I wished I could, because this was another reason they stood out as 'orphans' in school, apart from anything else. Penny and Cedric, my neighbours, told me of little differences like this, when I went to supper. They had friends who taught in the local school and were full of ideas of how to improve the children's lot. Penny was a wonderful cook and they proudly showed me their new television set and we ate vindaloo, watching their favourite soap - Hyacinth Bouquet on BBC.

On our way home from the Zoo another day it occurred to me that the boys had never been into a supermarket so we stopped and all went in. It was wonderful: Mukesh -the little, pointy eared boy from next door, led the way, and about ten of us went around the shop. They absolutely loved it, of course, were ever so well behaved. Mukesh, however, managed to leave five cash tills flashing at the checkout with their red lights blinking and their bells ringing and scores of people standing around with their mouths open at his dexterity.

Babu made my day by discovering *himself* reflected in a mirror and I think it might have been the first time he'd seen himself. He was standing in the middle of the tins of soup, nodding somewhat anxiously at first, and then smiling and waving at himself in the mirror. I made up my mind there and then to give my full-length mirror to the boys when I left. The rest of the boys solemnly inspected all the goods on the shelves and when I paid for a couple of things, the girl at the till offered me sweets to give to them all! It was when I was distributing these and talking to all the spectators that Mukesh did whatever it was that caused the tills to erupt.

On our return I had a long chat with a chap that helps in the Boys House. During our conversation he asked me how much I earned and whether or not I sent money home to feed my parents? Apparently that is what a lot of Indian men do - working in the Gulf or Canada for years sometimes. I didn't tell him I would be more likely to ask my parents to send *me* some money.

I was earnestly requested to attend the first Communion of one of the cooks' daughters. She wanted me to take some photographs. This mum arrived, beautifully dressed, to collect me at 7.30 a.m. and when we got to the Catholic Church there was a Band, The Bishop, hundreds of boys in spanking white trousers and shirts and hundreds of little, and big, girls awaiting communion looking more like brides in the sunshine. The Church was decorated with sparkly bunting and Christmas decorations and flowers and there was a huge colourful awning adjoining the main entrance to shelter the huge congregation of adoring parents from the boiling sun or pouring rain, both of which happened every day at that time.

I positioned myself behind some gladioli with a lovely vantage-point. A young assistant vicar helped me to climb to this rather precarious spot. He was dressed all in white and, I was fascinated to note, brown tights or popsocks under his sandals. However, no sooner had I felt like a foreign correspondent or a photo-journalist, and gloated privately about my position which would show the Bishop actually putting the bread in their mouths, than I realised there were at least thirty of these girls and I had only met the one I was to photo, once before. Which one was she? I waited for the film to be developed with great anxiety. I had taken at least five photos of the one girl that gave me a cheeky grin as she approached His Holiness, and fervently hoped that she was The One.

I was still only half friendly with the little white cat, which I thought prevented the Rat returning to my house. He/she did get on my nerves a bit. One night he overturned the milk yet again, that had just been delivered to the kitchen. While I was mopping it up, she ate my dinner off the table in the other room! When I moaned to Shanthi about the problem and complained that the cat was getting on my nerves, she said I should try drinking basil tea - which would be good for my nerves. Indian people are very hot on giving you advice for all aspects of Life and always have a solution to your problem - often from a point of view you hadn't expected.

During another Zoo Expedition, a couple of ex-Volunteers from Maldon, Essex, joined me, called Merv and Anne. They were Special Needs Teachers and an absolute mine of information about children with learning difficulties etc. On this expedition it was nice to have the stares from the Indian people diluted a bit. That day they had all our boys plus a couple of the Special Boys, and three 'foreigners' to look at, as we went around the Zoo. It was such a frantic day out, though, and I always seemed to do something silly in the extreme heat of the moment. On that particular day, I was calling out to one boy to give up his seat on the miniature train to another boy whose friends were carrying him on to the train. (They happened to be tiny and their friend a hulk). However, the boy I was entreating to get up burst out laughing because he was sitting on the seat because he himself had no useful legs, either. His friends had only just deposited him on the seat when I told him to get up for the other boy.

Oh dear, I wasn't going to moan about this, but my mosquito bites went bad and I wore brown gungy ointment for three days but they didn't clear up. In spite of this ghastliness, I was still healthy and supremely happy. When I was walking miles to get the Indian Sunday paper and three bottles of Pepsi, I realised I had stopped fantasising about the Sunday Independent and a chilled bottle of white wine and was totally content with the substitutes.

I also realised that my spirits soared at the thought of an adventure to another part of India and I was really excited about the next week when I would visit MYSORE. The pharmacist next-door-but-one had persuaded me that I must see his hometown before I returned to England.

I had to put a second coat of red paint on my bathroom floor, before leaving though, didn't I? Well, I thought it would be nicely dry for when I got home. It looked a treat and you couldn't see where I had left unpainted feet 'holes' in the wet paint so that I could still go to the loo until I painted them out at the last minute. The cheery red colour complemented the yellow walls and drew much admiration from the boys.

Anthony Williams Jackson - the son of Mary, the supervisor at the Boy's House - called for me as arranged in his auto-rickshaw. He would take me to the bus stop in Coimbatore where the Mysore bus stopped. In my new Nepalese salwar khameez I felt excited and pleased to be going away for a couple of days holiday. Anthony nearly flattened a policeman on the way and he was instructed by him to come off the road and into a lay-by. This policeman told me that the auto-car was unfit and that the MOT had expired and I should find alternative transport! Poor old Anthony got me another auto-car but the new driver didn't know the bus stop I needed to find for Mysore. I spent a horrid hour trying three different bus depots. Eventually another man and I ran to get the bus, which he said would take us to Mysore if we changed at somewhere unpronounceable. When I threw myself on the bus, which was going about twenty miles an hour - he *didn't* get on. I called out "Where do I change?" - he called back "You don't. It is going to Mysore."

Anyway, it was a lovely six-hour journey and not too uncomfortable - meaning nothing fell on me from above and the seats held together for the journey - and it *did* go to Mysore. A lot of people were lying up the aisle, including a little boy who did a bright yellow poo neatly beside himself, on the floor, in his sleep. Well everyone climbed over it, lifting their saris and passing their luggage to each other to avoid it, and complaining loudly. When the father called out from his seat at the front, to complain to the mother at the back of the bus about it, she got out at the next stop. She collected up a huge, dryish, cow poo, which she bought back into the bus, scooped up the baby poo in it and threw both poos out of the window.

There was the usual wonderful feeling of India passing the window. Paddy fields like 'mirrors' of water, trees with 'Tarzan' ropes hanging from them and wonderful buffaloes working the fields. The bus ran out of ooomph on uphill hairpin bends - all eleven of them - but it got us to our destination eventually. At the coffee stop a man sent me a Pokra (cashew nuts in floury batter, deep-fried) and another kindly man came up to mention to me that the bus was going without me. I was so busy noting the waiters who were all of eight years old that I hadn't noticed the other passengers were All Aboard. My years as a 'truancy man' made me very nosy about child labour and there was plenty of it for me to worry about in India.

Another lady on the bus must have had her suspicions about me because, seeing me scratching my head, she launched into a recipe for getting rid of nits - Anti-Lice-Juice she called it - in impeccable English. Apparently you add two tablespoons of lemon juice to two tablespoons of ginger juice and rub it into your scalp. Then you cover your head in muslin cloth for the night and in the morning they are gone. I can't believe it works because those ingredients were readily available here, and cheap, but you saw people sitting on every doorstep, combing through each other's hair to get rid of them. They were always recurring in the Orphanage but the girls vowed that it was one of their most favourite occupations, so perhaps that was why the recipe was not widely known.

Mysore was wonderful. I easily found a hotel for 124 rupees, (less than £3), and a tourist bus tour which went from 8 a.m. to 8 p.m. and took me to all the best temples, palaces, summer palaces, art galleries, a huge dam, and two lovely floodlit gardens. I could see St. Philomena's Church miles before we drew up outside it, and it looked so incongruously English - a huge grey familiar shape. When we were ushered in the door there had been an electricity cut (were they *following* me?) but the guide insisted we file down into The Tomb to 'see' St. Philomena. Well it was absolutely pitch dark but just to keep the guide lady happy, I took a flash picture - pointing my camera wildly in the direction she pointed. What do you think? It is the best picture of the 24 that I took that day. There she lies; a pink recumbent sari-ed lady, dead (sorry) centre of the picture.

I met two Belgians "You'll never be the same again, after India" and two Dutch women "We'll come and see you next week in your Orphanage" and one Edinburgh University student with a sister in Norwich, doing her Ph.D. in Indian History and wishing her mother would do what I am doing. Her mother is at that 'empty nest' stage that I never got over.

At the hotel I ate paneer masala (very thick yoghurt, cubed and deep fried, and plunged in a heavenly curry sauce, mushroom fried rice, Hyderabadi Chicken (divine), and fish in chunks. The table was lit by scooped out tomatoes with nitelites inside which gave a magical effect to the tree-lined terrace dining room. Three glasses of heavenly, glorious beer added to the luxury of course. The waiter was kind enough to provide an anti-mosquito 'coil', which he lit down by my feet before they started nibbling. Isn't it odd how they always make for your feet and ankles?

At the Brindavan Dam the next day I was surprised and delighted to see about fifteen enormous iron 'things' which made the dam work, and they had Ransomes and Rapier, Ipswich, England, 1924 stamped on them in huge letters. Ipswich is my hometown so I wanted to stop the Indian tourists to explain why I was so delighted with the dam workings. There were wonderful flowery gardens attached to the dam but I didn't know until later that there were musical fountains, too, and that the flowers were floodlit at night.

The Zoo in Mysore was less horrible than the one at Coimbatore. One of the attendants let me climb on a wall to take a picture looking right down a hippo's throat. He was less than pleased with me when I didn't tip him though - and I honestly didn't have any change. I sort of scurried away with a red face to examine the wonderful flamingos at a distance from the pool, while he waved his arms about and told the other visitors what a mean old biddy I was.

The bus for the return trip was different to the one coming, in that it had no springs and no lights. It kept plunging into holes and hitting rumble strips and boulders, and pitching me up in the air on the back seat. I had chosen to lie there thinking that I could sleep all the way home but by 5.30 a.m. when we arrived at the bus station, I was a battered wreck. However, a friendly little Indian doctor who was sitting half way up the bus saw me intermittently raised horizontally above the tops of the seats and walked back to talk to me nearly all night. He was about 25 years old and talked of his forthcoming arranged marriage to a dentist. He was most interested in the Orphanage and said he would come and visit and also tell his father to donate money to us. He said he thought his father should do this instead of giving money to 'silly old temples', so I hope he did.

9th August and William, my grandson's, third birthday. All the boys in Boys House sang Happy Birthday to his photo, and I gave them all a crayon to celebrate with him, in the morning. Then at suppertime, the two visiting Special Needs teachers toasted him in Pepsi and Sue-Sheila made us rice, poppadoms, curry sauce over fish and baby aubergines. We had a candle shaped like a three to complete the celebrations.

The friendly pharmacist offered me more brown gungy stuff for my mosquito 'holes' instead of gentian violet, which I eventually succeeded in banning from the Orphanage. Michael, the Canadian paediatrician gave me the authority to do this   he says it does nothing for anything, and I am hopeful that brown gunge will clear me up and solve the similar ills for the children instead of the gentian violet. The English couple couldn't believe I'd kept so fit all this time and the mosquito holes were my only complaint. They had had numerous dysentery attacks etc. and their anecdotes of previous trips were peppered with, 'Oh, that was when you had to go to hospital, or that was when we had to go home early because of this or that'. They made me feel like a tough old rhinoceros or something. I loved them being with me because they were so informative to the staff (and to me), with their professional knowledge of caring for handicapped kids. We were having his conversation about health matters and it was interrupted from time to time by about a dozen boys peering in the window and shouting, "Balloon Mummy!" We had given some out a few, earlier that day, for prizes for something and they were hopeful that I had more, but I didn't, I'm afraid.

Shanmurgan (by now a horrendously pimply and dribbly boy) had a birthday and for the first time in Special Care, they celebrated it with him. He was given a biro that he proudly put in his shirt pocket. He was about 17, going on 73, and clutched his birthday card so hard that the sparkly stuff transferred on to his face and stayed there all day.

I didn't know what to expect of the Fourth Academic Sports and Games Meeting arranged by the Tamil Nadu Police Traffic Wardens Organisation in a large town near to the Orphanage. At 1.30 p.m. a van-full (and I mean full) and a bus party set off for the town with Sunbeam, Anne and Merv, and six of the Orphanage staff. Mani the Driver returned to collect Marimuthu in his wheelchair and we all waited in the stadium for three hours for the events to start. Thirty ice-lollies helped a bit.

The Disabled Track Events were over-run (pardon the pun) with our Athletes. They wiped the board: First, Second, and Third time and time again. They raced over finishing lines to the amazement of onlookers and the wrath of other schools. The other schools tried devious tricks like putting the same children in for second and third times. Our children had never attended these Sports before and caused such a stir.

The photographs may not be too good as this photographer was definitely 'soggy'. The Tannoy system kept announcing things like '25 metres for Mentally Retarded Girls'. All our darlings would leap off in all directions at the start and still manage to come in First. One lad, Thangeraj raced proudly in a pair of pink shorts that we found hanging in the Gents when he got there too late to save his own from being wet. I don't think the real owner would have claimed them back after he had raced either.

Anne, Merv and I kept clapping the kids on the back and congratulating them when they were sitting in the lines of those who had come in the top three. We kept sticking our thumbs up and praising them every time they put one finger up to indicate they were First. However, someone told us eventually that this sign really meant that they needed to be Urine-Going!

The prizes were wonderful: chocolate, beakers with water lined-sides with moving pictures inside, and pencil boxes like bars of chocolate. Everyone got something, much to Mukesh's delight, as he hadn't come anywhere but had been sitting proudly with the children that came First, anyway.

All the children behaved wonderfully and were delighted with their day out, even before the Olympic style Parade that followed the prize giving. The teachers and carers were absolutely superb, endlessly moving the kids about in the stadium, up steps and ramps, on to the track, waiting nearly an hour for the transport and putting up with the traffic congestion on the way home. They never complained and kept up unflagging, enthusiastic encouragement and care for the kids all day.

The Procession and Cultural Happenings, as the Parade was billed on the programme, were like nothing I've ever seen in England. There were flags being marched, cyclists slow biking, and schoolchildren showing the clothes and dancing styles of Rajustan and Tamil Nadu. There were bands playing and people cartwheeling and handstanding and such an air of fun and carnival spirit.

At the end of this Parade, Superman Mani, the Driver, did his bit by gradually getting everyone home in relays in our old van because no bus turned up for us. At the start of proceedings, he had ensured a splendid vantage point for Marimuthu, who sat in his rusty old wheelchair, looking like an old Indian General taking the salute. Another thirty lollipops kept us all going on the journey home and the kids were already arranging who would take part next time.

The Indian doctor I talked to all night on the Mysore bus turned up on a motorcycle, one day. He had said he would like to visit the Orphanage, and to persuade his father to donate money to it, instead of to worthless old temples, so I took him on a tour of the Boys' House, Special Boys, Girls' House and Special Girls, and the Babies Room, of course. He was very emotional about it all and I don't honestly think he had visited anywhere like it before. He became tearful a couple of times and said he thought the staff were all saints. He promised to put an article in his Bombay medical paper where he works, to try and get us some money.

When he came back to my house for a pot of tea, he was most interesting about his arranged marriage. His prospective in-laws were buying his fiancée a practice (she is a dentist) and his own parents will buy him a medical 'centre', next door, when they marry. He had only seen this girl twice when I first met him so I asked if they had met since then. He said they had 'taken tea' together but she had cried most of the time - because he had teased her by saying he had spent the night on the bus with a beautiful foreign woman. I left him in no doubt as to what the beautiful woman thought of his crassness.

The photographs of the Sports day were OK after all, and one of them was particularly wonderful because it shows Mohammed 'flying' along in a race. Mohammed has a hunched back and cannot really walk or run without enormous difficulty, but the photo shows only him and he appears to be leaping ahead of everyone at speed and he was thrilled to bits with it.

I am sorry to say I failed at Yoga. I was so excited about this five-evening course, which covered meditation, relaxation and fitness. The teacher, called Divyanandra, was an eccentric American woman, about my age, and a good friend of Indira. When I found her 'studio' she welcomed me clad completely in orange garments. She was tall, fit and thin and very American and friendly. She loved me for some reason and I was anxious to do everything she said correctly. At first I thought I had this teensy headache while doing the exercises, because of some strong coffee I'd had. We'd been instructed to fast for several hours before we came, as well. The other participants were a mixture of men and women who all looked a bit tense and worried about the whole thing. The music and instructions were very gentle and felt therapeutic rather than strenuous, and everyone managed to do the leg-waving-about bits without strain. Someone passed wind and that helped things along a bit because I started to laugh and they joined in.

A rather hairy-faced lady next to me had the loudest rumbling tummy I ever heard, too, so I had to urgently think of other things to stop laughing and concentrated on the music and contortions suggested by Divyanandra.

I developed a really thumping, horrible, headache at the next night's session but I still hoped it was just coincidence. The other people had become more relaxed and friendly and had got over their initial curiosity - and suspicion - of me and it was quite a jolly session but I felt awful again.

Then the third night I was so unwell I had to come out of the lesson half way and fall in a café and drink three cups of Indian (thick, sweet) coffee until I stopped shaking. Well Divyanandra was disappointed, too, but she said some people do react like that. I think her methods and exercises must be a lovely way to relax and get fit but it certainly didn't suit my body for some reason. The mystery is that I was certainly the oldest and yet possibly the fittest person there. Divyanandra thought this, too, and suggested 'the toxins were focussed following some undiagnosed ailment'. I haven't a clue what that meant. I didn't seem to suffer any ill-effects from the effort I had made to become fit and relaxed and went back to feeling my usual slobby self, and looking pretty much the same, too. I had forgotten about what I looked like with my new hair cut, but Ghandi (the Social Worker) said he wanted to mention it to me one morning in the office, but he thought he might laugh, so he'd left it until that night.

Indira asked me to another wedding and I accepted the invitation with alacrity - they amaze me with their glamour and expense and opulence and I loved hearing about the emotional and traumatic difference that marriage entails in India. This wedding was of the girlfriend of a relative of Indira's and I was only invited because I was from England, I am sure. However, I was made predictably welcome and took some photographs and talked my head off to family and friends because I now knew it was expected of me. The bride, who was sitting in an emerald green sari, crying softly, gave us a sort of audience, while she had her hair combed by her sister. The tears are a normal part of the day, and I was again told that, even if the husband or his family *beat* the wife, she can't go home because it would bring shame on her own family.

At home the little cat still lived with me on and off and kept The Rat away as far as I could tell. She woke me one morning by being noisily sick and I had just gone back to sleep when Anthony, the old man in the hut next door, began his throat clearing exercises - from feet internally upwards. He then emerged from his hut with a tin can and scooped his shaving water out of a 'missionary/cannibal' pot that was full of boiling water on a brightly flaming fire of coconut husks. This water was warmed for the boys next door to wash in, and he collected some daily for himself. He had a toothbrush sticking out of his mouth and wore only a tiny pair of luminous green pants. He was about

Ghandi's wedding

seventy, fit and wiry, and he was hung with huge wooden crucifixes and other baubles. He just removed his toothbrush long enough to say, "Morning, Mummy" to me, and disappeared into his hut again. I continued making my omelette and mused on the differences between my neighbours here and those at home.

What I had thought was going to be a chat to the Social Work section of a huge local College, turned out to be a 'Lecture by a Distinguished Foreign Lecturer' to fifty postgraduate girls who bulged with intellect and awaited with interest and misplaced optimism to hear how English people counsel disabled people and their parents.

'Madam Jenny' stepped on to a rostrum with full amplification provided, and survived to tell this tale, only because they were absolute darlings and loved role-playing. They took the roles of counsellor, distracted parent and physically disabled child with great aplomb and they asked dozens of sensible questions. One of the girls gave me 100 rupees for the Orphanage, and then another particularly lovely girl thanked me formally and said they wished more lecturers were like me. I had a nice time.

Another, less demanding, invitation came following the Youth Group's visit. I was collected by a boy to go to lunch with his mother, who I had met at the Concert in Boys' House. However, he came for me on a motorbike and I had to decline the lift as I had no insurance. He agreed to accompany me on the bus instead, talking all the time about how 'agile' I was, compared with his mum. Talk about ego boosting. However, I explained that I had had a 'slobbing about' type of life and it had not been like that of Indian women. I reminded him of the fact that they rise at 5am, cook, clean, get everyone off to work and school, often work in their 'day jobs' in high degrees of heat as coollie, nurse, ayah, teacher, and then return home to cook and clean again. Add to this the necessity of wearing of miles of impossibly hot material and carrying pounds of thick hair right down their backs and standing on buses with hundreds of people and - and - and - well when I described my English life, he got the message.

We lunched in his house, which was more like an English home, being in the middle of Coimbatore and belonging to a dual-salaried couple. We used our hands to eat lunch, but sat up to a table, which is apparently normal now in middle-class Indian homes. I was given a velo lesson - a sort of giant mandolin, and questioned minutely about life in England and my own family. All the women cried when I left because they wouldn't see me again! I wasn't tearful, for once, because as I left the house, an aunt came visiting to try out her scooter driving. She had a new vehicle with specially covered wheels for sari wearing women. She hadn't learned the bit about brakes though and kept using her feet. It was definitely a case of "Wheeeee look where it is taking me now" when she took off. I was impressed that she dared to ride it because it is still considered improper for Indian women to sit *astride* anything. I supposed she *could* nip her knees together going along.

I was worried at this time about Raji's brother. She told me he was in hospital with typhoid as a result of drinking the local water. He had lost kilos in weight and still had a high fever and could not eat. Everyone seemed quite philosophical about it though, and said that he could come home after a couple of days in hospital. Before I knew all this I had forgotten my initial warnings and misgivings about the water and cleaned my teeth twice daily under a running tap. I speedily returned to religiously using sterilised water after hearing about Raji's poor old brother.

CHAPTER FIFTEEN

A weekend away, a visit from 'Irish' Jane and I vet some prospective in-laws

I decided to go to see the Indian friend of an English friend in Cochin for a long weekend. Mary George was the wife of a Minister in Ipswich but he had died and she had returned to her home in Kerala. She, and my English friend Sandra, were most anxious that Mary and I meet and although I really didn't think I could spare the time, I didn't want to lose the opportunity to meet her, and Sandra would've been disappointed if I hadn't made the effort. It was only about four and half hours on the train from my house to Kerala.

On the morning that I had arranged a visit to see Mary, I walked alone to the station at Podanur, about half a mile, much to the consternation of Sunbeam who feared for my safety. I assured her that any menacing, evil men lurking on my route, would have jumped in the bushes to avoid me, because I am so much taller and fatter than the average resident, and in the poor light at 5 a.m. and with my big hat on, I think I would have scared any of them.

There was wonderful scenery all the way to Kerala - which means Land of Coconuts. My seat on the train was tiny, there was a great crush of people and the window was obstructed, though, so I was anxious not miss the Cochin stop. I hoped it would be clearly marked and it was but clearly marked 'Ernakulum', which *means* Cochin.

148

I ignored this sign, of course, and when the train touched the buffers after another hour, I realised I had overshot and had to be rescued by a lovely man. He was called John Matthew and he said he recognised me, when I leaned out of the carriage, as being a Protestant Christian and told me that the Lord had sent him to guide me. With that introduction, I felt I could ignore my mother's advice about going off with strange men, and I happily went with him in an auto-rickshaw and on a bus. He eventually put me in the charge of another man in another bus, telling him (I suspect) to put this loopy woman out at a certain stop. John Matthew and I said goodbye and my new guardian promptly went to sleep. However, I managed, after travelling in two more buses and an auto-rickshaw, to be delivered right to Mary's door. She was amazed and delighted she had been waiting for me to telephone her as arranged and would have collected me from Cochin station. She lives in such a remote area that no visitor from England had ever simply knocked on her door before.

The house, garden and surrounding countryside were exotic. The locals hired elephants to do heavy work in their gardens and I saw elephant 'leavings' that you had to climb over in Mary's road, as well as an elephant working in her neighbour's garden. How I *love* that animal. The flowers, trees and bushes were so tropical and 'vulgar' and prolific that I couldn't get over them. I saw rice crops, rubber trees, banana plantations, black pepper bushes, cinnamon trees, gorgeous butterflies, cardomums, mangos, papaya, Japanese roses, sort of pink, hanging down sycamore seed pods, hibiscus, bougainvillaea and many more exotic plants and flowers and most of these grew in Mary's garden.

Mary was wonderful. I hope I have joined her legion of worldwide friends. I loved her. She and her little companion/help made me wonderful things to eat and drink for two days and nights and I felt like a big old cuckoo being looked after by little birds. I had wonderfully quiet nights and early mornings for the first time for months *and* a mattress that wasn't coconut husks. Mary took me round the village to meet all her friends and many relatives, and the Minister, and we looked round her Church. This was a very, very simple Church, unlike most other Roman Catholic Churches I have seen, and there were large doors which were wide open on each side, and through which you saw the night sky, which was the most wonderful colour, with coconut trees silhouetted against it. Noises of different birds and insects, and the bell tolling the hours, were the only sounds. Incredible, I thought.

We went to visit a Boys' Home, funded by Germans, which was near the Church. Just as we arrived the electricity supply had been cut off so I made the suggestion that we postpone our visit to another time. The poor supervisor had 70 boys to feed, no help and no lights, and I knew from personal experience that visitors would not be nice for him! We returned the next day as arranged and it was then lovely, for me particularly, as they spontaneously sang a regional song and the Supervisor was so happy to show us around. The boys were so unselfconscious and showed me their drawings and schoolbooks with pride. Then we toured the accommodation and I took their photographs and it was a lovely visit.

I was interested to note that whenever I visited an Orphanage or a Home or Hostel which was funded by overseas charities, there seemed to be a 'flavour' of the country the funds come from. The Home for Fallen Women, for example, funded by Swedes, was all samplers and tapestries and bleached pine and blue and white decor. This Boys Home was very clinical and 'organised' and regular - even the garden in the tropical temperature and relatively wet atmosphere, was *ordernung* and German.

Meanwhile, at Mary's house, she was still making me things like Idiappayd, which was a sort of Allbran cake with ground coconut on top and cashew nuts and raisins in hot goat's milk. We had Chicken Supreme, not a bit like my recipe, and curried yoghurt sauce and egg roast. Cinammon tea was lovely, sticks boiled in water with ordinary tea leaves added and left to cool. The water was from her well and was delicious. Fish cutlets were made from haddock and mixed with chopped leaves and dipped in rice batter. Some, to Western eyes, ghastly blue netting was purchased from a man coming round to the doors. The colour was so offensive in the lovely tropical surroundings but was eagerly bought to protect the wells from leaves. Mary bought some metres of it for three pounds and draped it over the well. It amused me to see him ask for a knife to be brought from the house to cut it off the roll - he didn't have any tools. Mary bought him the huge sabre that she had used to make a wonderful carved pineapple dessert with, the night before. It is obviously a valued item in an Indian household.

On the day of my departure, we breakfasted in Mary's nearest town at a sort of charity tea-room that she runs. She ordered vegetable stew for me for breakfast but (happily!) that wasn't available so she ordered Bulls Eye instead. I was a bit nervous about that, too, but it was an incompletely fried egg on white sliced bread, which was a little easier to manage than her first choice. Mary even managed to press on me Bombay Mix, packets of Mango cream biscuits and a bag of very sweet rice stuff wrapped in cones of filo-like pastry for the journey! She was so kind and we had a very tearful farewell at the station.

My journey home was funny. Seven people travelled in a carriage for four, lying down and fast asleep. One had another's smelly feet right next to his head, and they were not relatives or anything. One smoked the incredibly nice-smelling cigarettes. One had an extremely long smallest fingernail. I think this is a Muslim thing, as several men had it and also sported coloured nail polish on all their nails. All the passengers gave me space and I could see clearly out of the windows this time, and once again thoroughly enjoyed an Indian train journey.

Coming 'home' was lovely. All the boys were so pleased to see me and there was a great pile of post from England, including photos of Holly and William on holiday at Sheringham. I have to admit to being very Post-Dependent - it is like having a Hoggar Helpline - and I was so pleased to hear everyone's news and re-establish contact in this way. Two tomatoes in my garden pots had ripened and I had a white rose bud on my bush. I was touched that the children had not taken them.

My last visitor arrived - an ex-Volunteer called Irish Jane (by me, to differentiate between her and my own daughter Jane). She was from Tipperary but spoke 'proper' English. She was about 26 years old, full of beans, and one of those people you felt you have always known and loved. She said she was impressed with the 'garden' around my house and I must say it was looking good by then. I had been 'helped' with it by the boys next door who watered it when I asked them and when I didn't. It had often been submerged in water for days on the trot and then left until the earth cracked in the drought! In spite of this, there was a healthy bush at the entrance to my house, and a fairly healthy creeper against the walls, as well as several pots of roses, tomatoes and honeysuckle.

Irish-Jane was another valuable historian for me. She told me in detail about the time when the Volunteer was sent home for riding on the elephant - and, more happily, of the fun she had when she was here with a group of young Volunteers. I felt a bit envious of their larking about with the Orphanage boys and girls - throwing ice cubes at each other etc. and felt that the children must have found me a sober old biddy in comparison.

Jane was troubled about *callipers*. The children that came for exercises with the physiotherapists every day, should apparently have been wearing the callipers that were ordered and delivered in Jane's day but they had 'gone missing' since then. Apparently they had been sent for repair but the shop closed mysteriously and they were never seen again. Jane was so disappointed to see no progress in the children's mobility since she was here last. There is a diversity of opinion as to whether it is worth the children persevering with the blooming things anyway, because they get about quite quickly, crawling. However, I think I side with Jane in that the dignity of being upright is a valuable and worthwhile reward for the effort of the exercises. She pursued the whole subject with enthusiasm but I didn't envy her, finding the whereabouts of the old callipers, or obtaining funds for new ones was not going to be an easy task.

She had more luck with solving a rather nasty problem that she felt *she* caused at Girls' House - in the loo. She had cause for an emergency call there herself, and was relieved (!) to find a Western style toilet in there. However, after trying to flush it, unsuccessfully, it erupted *upwards* with the most horrible consequences. She raced ahead of the disgusting, eddying and swirling ghastliness and shut the outside door and raced to tell Sunbeam. The office people all calmed her and said they would call The Plumber, so Jane came home and tried not to feel guilty about causing the catastrophe. The next day, however, when she saw The Plumber, she went into shock again. The Plumber was the tiniest little Indian woman you have ever seen and was the *mother* of one of the ayahs in Girls' House. However, she had apparently calmly altered the Western system to an Asian style toilet - she threw away the Western lavatory, leaving just the hole in the ground!

Before I left for Cochin I was asked to be part of a quorum needed to check on the suitability of the family of a boy who wanted to marry one of our girls, Vanitha, in Girls House. She had been 'asked for' by the Ganesh Family. It was the first time this had happened at the Orphanage and, apart from a sort of feeling that she had been chosen like you'd choose a puppy from a pet shop, it was all very exciting and romantic, I thought. Sunbeam, Mr. Suami, Ghandi and I went by car to a remote village and were met

153

in the centre of the village by the prospective brother-in-law. He guided us on his bicycle to their home, which was in the middle of nowhere. After leaving our shoes at the door, we were welcomed into a long, low, earth-floored room, with plastic chairs, a birdcage full of training shoes, some bedding resting on poles, and a very new and large coloured television.

I couldn't help noticing the very loud shampoo advertisement showing on their television. The long, shiny hair swinging about on an Englishwoman, accentuated the difference from my own "crew-cut" so I kept it hidden by my sun hat, hoping they weren't disillusioned about Englishwomen.

I had been warned not to wear black for this meeting because that is a sad colour. Red meant accidents and bad things - like blood - but happily the violet salwar khameez I was wearing that day was deemed appropriate by Sheila in Girls House. I had discussed the significance of colours with her early that day. She had conjunctivitis and warned me that as our eyes had been in contact, I would be getting conjunctivitis very soon! I'm happy to say I didn't.

Mr. Suami requested the television be quietened and the negotiations began. The sweet, calm and smiling prospective ma-in-law gave us coffee and bananas and coconut sweets and a 26 year old, 'Omar Sharif' lookalike who was the prospective groom, and his father, answered our questions. Father had huge brown eyes, and big, white and red Hindu forehead markings. They established that the family would not mind if Anita had a Christian ceremony as well as their Hindu one, but ascertained that no one need convert to Christianity in *their* family. Whether or not Vanitha kept on her job was up to her, but they would like her to live at their home. Sunbeam told me that Vanitha worked at the same place as Garnesh so they had seen each other a lot, but apparently had not spoken yet. The mother-in-law to be and other members of the family had already visited the Orphanage to discuss the gifts and clothes which the Orphanage would give the Garnesh family and these arrangements were confirmed.

The reception would be held - and paid for - by the Orphanage but the Garnesh family would have a Hindu celebration in their home as well. Auspicious dates were discussed and it was decided that September or October, before Divali, would be a good time for them both.

We were offered some green leaves and packets of something else unknown to me, but I never got around to trying them because we were whisked outside to admire their garden, the ready supply of firewood and the healthy vegetables growing outside. We walked to the van through eight feet high cactus trees and picked our way between black and white pretty beetles on the ground. There had been no handshaking or contract signing but I told them that if Vanitha didn't want to live with them, I wouldn't mind! They all laughed merrily and there was a lot of excited discussion among the Orphanage party, about the wedding, on the way home. I wished, yet again, though, that I'd mastered Tamil because everyone had got a bit fed up with translating by the end of the day, and I *did* want to hear their opinions of everything but of course I couldn't keep asking what had been said.

CHAPTER SIXTEEN

Time to go home!

I was a bit shocked by the tears and agonising of the people here about my departure. Irish Jane had explained that they are always like it. I thought my sister and I were the only ones to cry whenever we say goodbye, but there is a whole Continent of big brown eyes that fill with tears, and sob at the mention of people leaving. Irish Jane went to say goodbye to the girls on the morning of her departure, and I arranged to carry her rucksack and walk to meet her later at the station. In this way I could avoid all their tears. However, one of the boys saw me walking past Boys House and carrying Jane's rucksack, thought *I* was leaving, and fell in a heap, crying and wailing - honestly.

I seriously thought of slipping off a couple of days early to avoid the trauma. Sunbeam had kindly spread the word that I definitely did NOT want a Function for my farewell. It was usual to have a 'do' and give gifts and hang garlands round the departing peoples' necks but I persuaded her I definitely could not cope with all that. I invited the office staff to a Goodbye Supper in town because I thought *they* would be calmer or perhaps glad to see me go. At any rate I didn't think they would *cry*.... and without the Function, I could slip away to England with a degree of dignity. It didn't quite work out like that but Sunbeam helped me avoid the disaster it would have been.

Before I left I had arranged for mural-painting Sam to paint more pictures at the entrance to Boys' House. We agreed that a man and a boy on one side of the inner door, and a woman and a girl on the other side would be appropriate. Then at the outer door the Canadian flag would be painted on the right hand side, and the Indian flag on the left. I had a feeling it might look like the Family Planning Clinic for some reason - but if it did - well, hey, so what! Sam did a lovely job again and apart from wishing the Union Jack could have been incorporated, I was very happy with the effect.

My last social occasion in India had been a Gospel Night in the village and I clapped and halleluja-ed for an hour or two under a scarlet and orange sky and strip lights in the banana trees. I went with friends called Ebeneza, Abraham, Thebera (my friend the laundry maid) and Gracie and Priscilla. The Minister went on and on and on and when I recognised my only Tamil word ('yesterday') and realised that I probably wouldn't recognise any more words that night - I decided to come away. They didn't mind. I handed back a green woollie-clad baby with coconut-oiled skin and hair, who I had been cuddling and who had the most beautiful eyes in the world and I drifted 'home'. As I passed Boys' House I noticed they had erected a huge fence all round a pot of geraniums I had given them, to protect it from their footballs. You couldn't see the geraniums at all.

The last week had passed in a haze of taking everyone's photograph, crying, giving away everything that had been asked for in my apartment, crying, making promises to write to absolutely everyone and crying. The crying here is ghastly. I thought I was a crier, but Indians.

The boys kept giving me wonderful cards and pictures they had drawn of me in my big sun-hat with captions like: This is a Jenny Mummy, Big Mummy, Presentation by Polio Boys, Don't Cry/Be Happy, Wish You All Best, Polio Boys, as well as Indian messages that I wouldn't even ask to have translated, because they would have made me cry again...

On the last day of course I disgraced myself by kissing and hugging everyone - men and women. I *know* that Indians don't *do* that and the poor devils are probably still reeling from a fat, sweaty old woman grabbing men, women and children indiscriminately. Oh, I was *pathetic* but I just had to give them a hug, I loved them so much. They were worse than I was, even though they probably didn't want to hug and kiss. Their big brown eyes were full of tears and they wailed and cried - it was a *ghastly* day altogether. And the *presents!* Huge ornaments and New Testaments and big brass bowls and Revival Gospel tapes and a seagull suspended on an luminous pink stand. How was I to get them in my luggage, let alone on the 'plane?

Shanthi came to see me off with her little girl, Persil, and told me lurid tales to take my mind off the parting and stop me crying. I heard about her mother in law, who had given birth to twin boys, fell downstairs and died within two days of the delivery. And the story of the electrician and his baby, who I had photographed that day. His first little boy had died from diarrhoea and they didn't have a photo of him so that was why they had bought No. 2 Son to me that morning, to put him on record. I heard these stories and others, which entertained me until my train arrived. Shanthi had to yell these details, above the sounds of the hoards of other departing passengers.

The Invisible Benefactor, who had sent me gifts throughout the year, also came to see me off at the station bearing more gifts. He requested that I ring his friend in Finchley who has MS. He apparently ' also loves White Women, very much.'

Shanthi, and three or four men that were getting the same train, raced up and down looking for Seat No. F56 which was printed on my ticket. It turned out that the F56 meant I was a female aged 56 years. The three men said I had confused them. They got over it, though, and moved in with me and swapped anecdotes and family details for the next three days and nights until we got to Delhi.

I enjoyed their offering of betel nut breath freshener - betel nuts fried in perfume. A lady in the next carriage sent us some Golden Rice as a present, and they all helped me to choose my other meals sold on board, at regular intervals, and they were all delicious. Served on steel trays, at each station, there was lovely chicken curry, dhal, egg curry, omelettes and loads of hot sweet coffee. Lassi was served too - a sort of sugar cane extract mixed in yoghurt with fruit juice, cardamom and black pepper.

We talked of the differences in our two countries and I thought one man, Ali, was sweet as he described his people as 'Not Too Worried About *Clean*' ... Kumar told me about Divali being a celebration for which everyone had new clothes, bought tons of sweets and usually got a financial bonus at work. He also told me there are 25 varieties of Paan. Ali had a Ph.D. in Hindu and his English was excellent.

Three uniformed Indian policemen got in the carriage with rifles and told me the rifles were to protect the police salaries, which they carried in a huge tin trunk. The men didn't seem so threatening; when I looked at their FEET they either wore flip flops or big old shoes with no socks. They smoked cigarettes and chattered away to me - but there was not much conversation between each other in the carriage. I had noted this fact in India on several occasions. I mentioned the unreliability of train times in India and they assured me that in India if a train is even hours late, they reckon it is early for the next day.

The flight home was as interesting and exciting as coming out had been. I watched a fellow passenger sketch a wonderfully 'lined' gentleman of about eighty years, wearing a Sikh's turban. He was very aristocratic and regal but he chattered to anyone who would listen, about the ten minutes it takes to 'erect' the turban. It is moulded around one's head while wet and starchy and dries on your head. You can wear it more than one day if it is created like that. My fellow passenger/artist allowed her drawing to be passed around the plane for admiration, too. It was a very 'matey' trip but of course I was seething with excitement about seeing my family at Heathrow. I raced my trolley through customs, wearing my Nepalese knitted full-length

Back home!

coat of *very many* colours and one of those Nepalese hats with sort of plaits each side. My son said they had been watching a plane load of Russian women sweep through the door - all about six foot tall and wearing furs and elegant clothes and suddenly there was a 'knitted gnome', only five feet high, and it was his mummy. My darling daughter and niece were there, too, both looking even more beautiful, and they swept me into the café and 'lavished' me with pots of tea, bottles of beer and LOVE and it was everything a homecoming could be.

Wasn't that all an Adventure? I loved India and the Indians and especially the Orphanage staff and Boys and Girls. The Indian people love us and, if you go, will make you so welcome that you will be as pleased you went as I was.

You will have appreciated, by now, that I recommend everyone to go for an adventure *anywhere* - especially if you are my age. I can't say I *found* myself, exactly, because that is how other people have described similar experiences, but

I am happy to say that my assumption that travelling is good and exciting and people everywhere are going to be warm-hearted and friendly, was confirmed.

I didn't *find* myself but I learned to appreciate bits of myself that I had taken for granted before I left home. I have feelings of well-being and healthiness, which I thought everyone else, had. I know, since India that everyone doesn't have this good fortune - certainly in the humid and often uncomfortable conditions that Indians live in. Another aspect I have thought a lot about since India, is my new understanding of Do-Gooders Doing Good - I don't mind joining them now because there is a definite buzz to be had when you can avoid anyone you know *seeing* you Do Good. Without the self-consciousness I would have had in England, I *loved* staggering around with those boys in wheelchairs and lugging them up and down the stairs at railways stations. Am I funny? Do other English people have this 'hang-up'? When the Indians called out things to the effect that I would get Brownie Points when I died, I just laughed and agreed with them but the thought of what people in England would say about me, would prevent me doing anything. I don't think I'll go back to India yet because I'd so like to see other countries and meet more people of different opinions and outlooks but I think I am now equipped and capable of helping out in another country, perhaps teaching English or something. The Indian experience has confirmed my confidence in being on my own for long periods of time, and not getting on my own nerves (well, not much), or too lonely. I am sure I'll never settle for a couple of weeks' holiday anywhere, however exotic or wonderful. I think I am thoroughly English about the work ethic - feeling guilty if I am sitting or lying down in the daytime. I would be unhappy if I wasn't going to be in one place long enough to get to know the people and their customs in detail. I can understand the Volunteers' need to return to the orphanage in India, and hope that I, too, can surprise them one day. Their need is for advice and support from time to time and the staff and children all assured me that they long for visits from all their Western friends - both for their social and professional input as well as for donations.

P.S.

I have been home six years now, having spent time teaching in China, Mexico and Hong Kong. They were completely different adventures and China was even more taxing - physically and mentally - than India. But I will tell you all about that another day. In the meantime I must say - as always -

I'M SO PLEASED TO BE HOME, I'M GLAD I WENT!

The End